THE IPHONE 11 PRO

GUIDE

Your Complete iPhone 11 Pro Manual for

Beginners, New iPhone 11 Pro Users and Seniors

Tech Analyst

Copyright @2019

TABLE OF CONTENT

How to Use this Book

Welcome! Thank you for purchasing this book and for trusting us to lead you right in operating your new device. This book has covered every detail and tip you need to know about the iPhone 11 to get the best from your new smartphone.

To better understand how the book is structured, I will advise you read from page to page, after which you can then navigate to particular sections as well as make reference to a topic individually. This book has been written in the simplest form to ensure that every user understands and gets the best out of this book. The table of content is also well outlined to make it easy for you to reference topics as needed at the speed of light.

Thank you.

and it will show you recent messages, photos, people and other options. The search results tend to be more refined as you type to narrow down to the item you need.

Dark Mode

Once you update your device to the iOS 13, you will begin to enjoy the new dark mode features. The dark mode gives your phone a dark background and highlights on the phone's iOS and all the default Apple apps like messages, emails, and other apps. Apple has also asked developers to include this feature in third-party apps, and so, very soon, you will be able to enjoy this feature on other non-Apple apps. You have the option of either setting this mode permanently or modifying it to suit a particular time and period. You will see how to do this later in this book.

Photos and Cameras

The camera app now has a new feature known as **High Key Mono,** a lighting effect with the portrait camera mode. You can also decide how intense you want the light to be by using the editing features to make your skin look smooth and bright to the eyes similar to what you see done with the moving lights found in a studio. The image editing feature of the photo's app has a swipe-based control as well as a new design. Now, you can use the same settings you use for stills to also edit your videos. Not only that, you can now rotate videos and also add filters. The Photo library has also been equipped to discover and delete duplicate copies of a single photo while it selects the ones that Apple will regard as your best shots. The images are then organized by months, day, or year, and you can see them in a new album view.

Another addition is that the live videos and photos are now on autoplay in the new photos tab, and you can now see the event, location or holiday, etc. for that photo within this same tab. On the photo tab, you will also see the new birthday mode that allows you to view pictures of celebrants on their birthdays. Now, you will see all your screen recordings in a single place, which makes it more organized and saves time used in searching all over the app.

Accessibility

Permit me to say that the addition of voice control is the most significant accessibility change that we see in the iOS 13, and this feature makes it easy for you to control your smartphone using your voice. The Siri speech recognition algorithm is used to confirm that the sound belongs to the authorized user before allowing access to the phone. You can also include custom words of your choice. No need to worry about personal data as the system leverages on device processing to keep your details safe.

Improvement to FaceTime

The iOS 13 also brought some improvements to the FaceTime video calls, especially in positioning the eye while on calls. The FaceTime software makes use of ARKit first to scan your face and then softly modify your eyes' position in a way that it will seem as if you are making direct eye contact with your caller rather than just starring at your screen.

Privacy

Apple has always been known to be particular about the privacy of its users, and we did not expect any less for iOS 13. Following the new granular controls, you can now decide apps that should have access to your location data. When you launch an app for the first time, you will see the option to either allow the app to access your location only once or for all the times that you may need to use the app. Apps will no longer be able to access your location through Bluetooth and Wi-fi without your permission. You are now able to choose persons that can see the location details of your photos. Each time you attempt to share your photos through the photo app, you will select whether the receiver should be given access to view the location the photo was shot in or not.

Performance

You will experience better performance on the new iOS 13 than was available with previous versions. Apple's Craig Federighi stated during the presentation that there would be a 30 percent increase in speed when using the FaceID to unlock your device. Apps updates have also been cut down by 60% while the size of apps downloads will be smaller by 50%. You will also experience a faster speed when launching apps than before.

Warnings for Active Subscription

On an attempt to delete an app you downloaded via in-app purchase from the Apple store, you will get a notification alerting you of the active subscription. You can then choose if you want to continue with your action or not.

Find My

In this new software upgrade, we saw that the **Find My Friend** and **Find My iPhone** features were collapsed into a single app called the **Find My** app. With this app, you can even find Lost devices regardless of whether they are offline by making use of the phone's Bluetooth connection.

Animoji and Memoji

Several new features are now available for Animojis and Memojis like glasses, makeup, hats, jewelry, and being able to change the look of your teeth. Your character can even wear Airpods. On your device keyboard, you can quickly access default Memoji stickers that you can share on apps like WeChat, Messages, and Mails.

Health App

Every function available on the new Watch OS health app is also in the iPhone 11 and all iOS 13 devices, functions like menstrual cycle tracking and the activity trends. On the main app, you will see a summary view where your notifications will be displayed as well as a highlight section to show your health and fitness data over time. Through machine learning, the app can show you things that are very important to your personal life.

Sign in with Apple

You will enjoy using this feature as it is an easy and fast way for you to sign in to services and apps without the need to reveal your social media login details. This feature authenticates your sign-ins using your Apple ID while ensuring that you do not disclose your details. This new service uses the TouchID and FaceID as well as a 2-

factor authentication system. If you need to verify your login attempt into any app, Apple will create a random email address linked to your primary email address where the verification mail is sent and then redirected to your primary email address.

Apple Maps

Before now, the Apple map had limited functions for its users, unlike the Google map. However, there have been several alterations and additions like adding beaches, roads, buildings along with heightened details. There is also a new Favorite feature on your main screen, as well as organizing all your favorites and planned trips into a collection menu. We now have what Apple called the **Look Around,** just like Google's **Streetview,** so that you can see what a location looks like before you physically visit. You will learn how to use this feature in a later part of this guide. Another thing is that you can now share your ETA with your family and friends, receive updated flight information, real-time updates on the availability of public transportations, and the improved Siri navigation.

CarPlay

On your CarPlay app, you will notice the main screen called the **Dashboard,** where you will find controls for podcasts or music playback. You will also see basic maps information as well as control your HomeKit devices like garage door opener from this app. Apple Music is also modified to make it easy to find music. There is also a new calendar app to show a quick view of the day when embarking on a journey.

Reminders

You can now add in times, dates, and attachments into the reminders app. The app has also been integrated with the Messages app to allow both apps to communicate together. What this means is that whenever you set a reminder about a contact, this reminder will pop up the next time you message this contact. Siri has also been integrated into the reminders app. When typing words, Siri will give some related suggestions to what you are typing. Siri has also been configured to read out your reminders, and so, when chatting in the messaging app, Siri notifies you of things it assumes you should remember.

CHAPTER 1

Getting Started: How to set up your iPhone 11

Setting up your device is the first and most crucial step to getting started with your iPhone 11. Follow these steps for a seamless experience.

1. Firstly, you need to power on your device. To do this, press and hold the side button. Now, you will see **"Hello"** in various languages. The screen will present options to set up your device. Follow these options on the screen of your device.

   Note: From the Hello screen, you can activate the **VoiceOver or Zoom Option,** which is helpful for the blind or those with low vision.

2. A prompt will come up next to select your language and country/ region. You must choose the right information as this will affect how information like date and time etc. appears on your device.

3. Next is to manually set up your iPhone 11 by tapping **"Set up Manually."** You can choose the **"Quick Start"** option if you own another iOS 11 or later device and then follow the onscreen instruction. Proceed with the manual setup if you do not have any other iOS devices.

4. Now, you have to connect your phone to a cellular or Wi-Fi network or iTunes to activate your device and continue with the setup. You should have inserted the SIM card before turning on the phone if going with the cellular network option. To connect to a Wi-Fi network, tap the name of your Wi-fi, and it connects automatically if there is no password on the Wi-fi. If there is a

security lock on the Wi-fi, the screen will prompt you for the password before it connects.

5. At this stage, you can turn on the Location services option to give access to apps like **Maps** and **Find my Friends**. You can always turn off this option whenever you want. I have included a guide on how to turn on or off location services in a later part of this book.

6. Next is to set up your Face ID. The face ID feature allows you to authorize purchases and unlock your devices using the registered face. To set up a face ID, tap **"Continue"** and follow the instructions on the screen. You can push this to a later time by selecting **"Set Up Later in Settings."**

7. Whether you set up Face ID now or later, you will be required to create a four-digit passcode to safeguard your data. This passcode is needed to access Face ID and Apple Pay. Tap **"Passcode Option"** if you will instead set up a four-digit passcode, custom passcode, or even no passcode.

8. If you have an existing iTunes or iCloud backup, or even an Android device, you can restore the backed-up data to your new phone or move data

from the old phone to the new iPhone. To restore using iCloud, choose **"Restore from iCloud Backup"** or **"Restore from iTunes Backup"** to restore from iTunes to your new iPhone 11. In the absence of any backup or if this is your first device, then select **"Set Up as New iPhone."**

9. To continue, you will need to enter your Apple ID. If you have an existing Apple account, enter the ID and password to sign in. In case you don't have a current Apple ID or may have forgotten the login details, then select **"Don't have an Apple ID or forget it."** If you belong to the class that has multiple Apple IDs, you should choose **"Use different Apple IDs for iCloud & iTunes."**

10. To proceed, you need to accept iOS terms and conditions.

11. Next is to set up Siri and other services needed on your device. Siri needs to learn your voice, so you will need to speak a few words to Siri at this point. You can also set up the iCloud keychain and Apple Pay at this point.

12. Set up screen time. Screen time will let you know the amount of time you spend on your device. You can also set time limits for your daily app usage. You will find a detailed guide on how to set up screen time in a later part of this book

13. Now turn on automatic update and other essential features.

14. Click on **"Get Started"** to complete the process. And now, you can explore and enjoy your device.

How to Use the Buttons and Sockets on iPhone 11

Side button: This is the first button by the top right side of the phone, formerly called the **"Sleep/ Wake"** button. You use this button to power on the device and turn on the screen lock.

Silent Mode Key: This is the sliding key at the top left side of the device. You move this key either up or down to switch on or off the silent mode. When silent mode is on, you will not get any sound notification on your device.

Volume keys: These keys are used to increase or reduce volumes for calls, music, or adjusting the ring volume. You can also use it to mute an incoming call alert.

Camera lens: This function is for taking pictures or videos.

Lightning port: this is the socket at the bottom of the device used to charge the device or to plug in a headset for a handsfree call or to listen to music.

How to Charge the Battery for the iPhone 11

You need to charge your phone often to ensure its ready for use at all times.

- Connect the phone charger to a power socket and then connect the USB side to the lightning port at the bottom of the phone.
- To know that your battery is charging, you will see the battery charging icon displayed at the top of the screen.
- At the top right side of the screen, you will see your battery level. The more the colored section, the more power the device has and vice versa.

How to Extend the Device Battery Life

Some apps and services on the iPhone 11 draw lots of power, which will drain the battery life faster. You can turn on low power mode to reduce power consumption.

- From **Settings**, go to **Battery**.
- Move the switch beside **Low Power Mode** to the right to enable it.
- Return to Home screen.

How to turn on iPhone 11

The following steps will show you how to turn on the iPhone 11:

- Press the **Side** button until the iPhone comes on.

- Once you see the Apple logo, release the button and allow your iPhone to reboot for about 30 seconds.

- Once the iPhone is up, you will be required to input your password if you have one.

How to turn off iPhone 11

Follow the steps below to turn off your iPhone 11:

- Hold both the volume down and the side button at the same time.

- Release the buttons once you see the power off slider.

- Move the slider to the right for the phone to go off.

- You may also use the side and volume up button; the only thing is, you may take a screenshot in error rather than shutting down the phone, if not careful.

Going Home on your iPhone 11

- Regardless of where you are on your iPhone 11, to return to the home screen, swipe the screen from the bottom up.

How to Choose Ringtone on the iPhone 11

- From the Home screen, go to **Settings.**
- Click on **Sounds & Haptics.**
- Then click on **Ringtone.**
- You may click on each of the ringtones to play so you can choose the one you prefer.
- Select the one you like then click the "**< Back**" key at the top left of the screen.

- Slide the page from the bottom up to return to the Home screen.

How to Choose Message Tone on the iPhone 11

- From the Home screen, go to **Settings.**
- Click on **Sounds & Haptics.**
- Then click on "**Text Tone.**"
- You may click on each of the message tones to play so you can choose the one you prefer.
- Select the one you like then click the "**< Back**" key at the top left of the screen.

How to Set/ Change Language on iPhone 11

- From the Home screen, click on the **Settings** option.
- Select "**General**" on the next screen.
- Then click on **Language and Region.**
- Click on **iPhone Language** to give you options of available languages.
- Choose your language from the drop-down list and tap **Done.**
- You will see a pop-up on the device screen to confirm your choice. Click on **Change to (Selected Language),** and you are done!

How to Set/ Change Date/ Time on iPhone 11

- From the Home screen, click on the **Settings** option.
- Select "**General**" on the next screen.
- Then click on **Date & Time.**
- On the next screen, beside the "**Set Automatically**" option, move the switch right to turn it on.

How to Use the Control Centre

- From the right side of the notch, swipe down to view the control center.
- Click on the needed function to either access it or turn it on or off.
- Move your finger up on the needed function to choose the required settings.

How to Choose Settings for the Control Centre

- Go to **Settings**> **Control Centre.**
- On the next screen, beside the "**Access Within Apps**" option, move the switch to the right or left to turn it on or off.
- Click on **Customize Controls.**

- For each function you want to remove, click on the minus (-) sign.

- To add icon under **More Controls,** click on the plus (+) sign at the left of each of the icons you want to add.

- Click on the **'move'** icon beside each function and drag the function to the desired position in the control center.

- And you are done.

How to Create Apple ID on iPhone 11

- Go to the **Settings** option.

- At the top of your screen, click on **Sign in to your iPhone.**

- Choose **Don't have an Apple ID or forgot it?**

- A pop-up will appear on the screen, and you click on **Create Apple ID**.

- Input your date of birth and click on **Next.**

- Then input your first name and last name then click on **Next.**

- The next screen will present you with the email address option. Click on **"Use your current email address"** if you want to use an existing email or click on **"Get a free iCloud email address"** if you want to create a new email.

- If using an existing email address, input your email address and password.
- If creating a new one, click on the option and put your preferred email and password.
- Verify the new password.
- The next option is to select 3 Security Questions from the list and provide answers.
- You have to agree to the device's Terms and conditions to proceed.
- Select either **Merge** or **Don't Merge** to sync the data saved on iCloud from reminders, Safari, calendars, and contacts.
- Click on **OK** to confirm the **"Find My iPhone is turned on."**

How to Set Up Apple Pay
- First is to add your card, either debit, credit, or prepaid cards to your iPhone.
- Ensure that you are signed in to iCloud using your Apple ID.

- To use the Apple Pay account on multiple devices, you have to add your card to each of the devices.

To add your card to Apple Pay, do the following:

- Go to Wallet and click on ⊕
- Follow the instructions on the screen to add a new card. On iPhone 11, you can add as much as 12 cards. You may be asked to add cards linked to your iTunes, cards you have active on other devices, or cards that you removed recently. Chose the cards that fall into the requested categories and input the security code for each card. You may also need to download an app from your card issuer or bank to add your cards to the wallet.
- When you select **Next,** the information you inputted will go through your bank or card issuer to verify and confirm that you can use the card on Apple Pay. Your bank will contact you if they need further information to verify the card.
- After the card is verified, click **Next** to begin using Apple Pay.

How to check out with Apple Pay

After shopping and you need to make your payments at a checkout terminal, the steps below would guide you on how to check out using Apple Pay:

- Double-press the side button to open the **Apple Pay** screen.
- Look at the iPhone screen to verify the attempt with Face ID (or enter your passcode).
- Then place the iPhone 11 near the payment terminal.
- If you're using Apple Pay Cash, double-press the side button to approve the payment.

How to use Siri on iPhone 11

Apples' virtual assistant is a delight to work with, everyone loves Siri, and most of the time you spend with her involves getting an answer, but she can do more than answer questions.

How to Set up Siri on iPhone 11

To use Siri on your iPhone 11, you have to set it up like you set up the Face ID. Find below the steps to do this on your iPhone 11.

- Click on **Siri & Search** from the **Settings** app.

- Besides the option **"Press Side Button for Siri,"** move the switch to the right to enable the function.
- A pop-up notification will appear on the screen, select **"Enable Siri."**
- Switch on the **"Listen to Hey Siri"** option and follow the instructions you see on the screen of your iPhone. (To use Siri when your phone is locked, activate the **"Allow Siri When Locked"** option).
- Click on **Language** and select the desired language.
- Click on the **< Siri & Search** button at the top left of the screen to go back.
- Scroll and select **Siri Voice.**
- On the next screen, select **Accent and Gender.**
- Click on the **< Siri & Search** button at the top left of the screen to go back.
- Select **"Voice Feedback."**
- Choose your preferred setting.
- Click on **< Siri & Search** at the top left of the screen.

- Select **My Information.**

- Click on the contact of choice. If you set yourself as the owner of the phone, the device will use your data for various voice control functions like navigating home. You can create yourself on the contact by following the steps given in creating contacts.

- Select the desired application.

- Navigate to **"Search and Siri Suggestions"** and move the slider to the left/ right to turn on or off.

- Now Siri is set up and ready to be used.

How to Activate Siri on the iPhone 11

There are two ways to activate Siri on your iPhone 11.

- Voice option. If you enabled "Hey Siri," then you can begin by saying "Hey Siri" and then ask Siri any question.

- The second option is to use the side button. To wake Siri, press the side button, and ask your questions. Once you release the side button, Siri stops listening.

How to Exit Siri

To exit Siri, follow the simple step below.

- Press the side button or swipe up from the bottom of the display to exit Siri.

How to Use Cycle Tracking in Health

The health app allows you to do lots of things beneficial to your health, like the menstrual cycle tracking as well as tools to know your most fertile days and your due date. Follow the steps below to learn how to use the cycle tracking feature in the health app.

- Launch the health app.
- Click on **Search** and select **Cycle Tracking** from the displayed list.
- Click on **Get started**, then click on **Next.**
- The app will request a series of information like the duration of your period and the date the last one started.
- You also get to choose how you will like to track your period as well as confirm if you will want to receive notifications and predictions on your next possible cycle.

- Confirm if you want to be able to record spotting and symptoms in your cycle log as well as if you wish to have access to your fertility windows.

- After you have provided all the responses, you can then go back to the **Cycle Tracking** homepage.

- In the **Cycle Tracking** homepage, click on **Add Period** to input days of your last periods.

- You can also click on **Spotting, Symptoms,** and **Flow Levels** option to input more specific details.

How to Use the Find My App

In iOS 13, you will no longer see the Find My iPhone and Find My Friends apps as Apple collapsed both apps into a single app called **"Find My."** This new app allows you to find your missing devices as well as share your location with your loved ones and friends. The simple steps below will show you how to use the app

- Locate the **Find My** app on your home screen.

- Navigate to the **People** tab to see your current location.

- If you wish to send your location to contact, click on **Start Sharing Location.**

- Type the name of the contact you want to send your location.

To find your missing device,

- Go to the tab for **Device** to see all the registered Apple devices on your account.
- Select the missing device, and you will see the following options on your screen: *Mark As Lost,* **Get Directions** to the device, **remotely** *Erase This Device,* or *Play Sound.* Select the option that bests suit your needs.
- If the device is not connected to the internet at the time this action was performed, you can choose to receive a notification once the device comes online. To do this, click the **Notify Me** option

How to Use Sign in With Apple

Not so many of us are comfortable with using our Instagram login details to sign in to several apps. Now with this feature, you can quickly sign into apps without sharing your personal information. To know apps that support this feature, you will see the option displayed on the app's opening screen.

- Click on the option for "Sign in with Apple," you will get a prompt to log in to your Apple account.
- On the next screen, choose only the information you want the app developer to access.
- This feature allows you to decide to share your email address or not to share it.
- If you choose not to share your email, Apple gives you a random email address that will be linked to your Apple iCloud email address. Any email sent to this random address will be automatically forwarded to your registered email address while keeping your details private at the same time.

How to Use Screen Time

This feature helps you to monitor how much time you spend on your device. On the screen time option, you will see the complete details on the hours spent on your iPhone. To do this,

- Go to the Settings app on your device

- Then click on **Screen Time**

How to Set App Limits

If you think you spend a lot of time on your device, you can use the App Limit feature of the Screen Time to set the length of time you want to spend on certain apps. Follow the steps below to guide you.

- Go to the Settings app on your device
- Then click on **Screen Time**
- Navigate and click on **App Limits.**
- Then select **Add Limit.**

In iOS 13, you can now group similar apps with the same app limit. What this means is that you can bring Spotify, Twitter, and Fortnite together to have a combined total of 6 hours every day. As soon as the limit is exhausted, a splash will appear on your screen notifying you that the set limit is exhausted. You will also get the option to ignore the deadline for the remainder of the day or just for 15 minutes only.

The New Reminders App

The Reminders app has several modifications and additions. Before now, the app lacked some features that are in similar third party apps. In the steps below, you will learn how to explore and use the revamped reminders app.

How to Create a Reminder

- Launch the reminders app.
- Then click on **reminders** under **My List** heading
- Then select **New Reminders** at the bottom of your screen, on the left side.
- Fill in your details for the reminder.
- Then click **Return** on your keyboard to confirm your first reminder.

How to Add a New Task to the Reminders app

From the home screen of the reminder app, you can now see all the reminders you have at the moment, those due today as well as numbers contained in each list. If you want to add a new task to an existing list, follow the steps below:

- From the home screen of the reminder app, click on **All.**
- Then click the "+" button located underneath each category to add a new task

The app now allows you to add a reminder time or date, change the category for a task, or set up a reminder for a task when in a specified location. To achieve this, click on the desired tasks to launch the options, then click on the **'I'** icon in blue color and set as desired.

How to Add SubTasks

For projects or tasks that are complex or have several levels, you can add sub-tasks or create a multi-entry list to use for shopping, for instance. The steps below will guide you on how to create subtasks.

- Go to the desired task on your reminder app.
- Then click on the blue "i" icon to see the available options.
- Go down on the next screen and click on **Subtasks.**
- Then click on **Add Reminder** to include a subtask.

- You can add as many subtasks as you want in a single task.
- You can locate the subtask in the reminder app or click on the main task.
- You can complete the subtasks without completing the parent task.
- You can also click on the **"i"** icon to add its own time, separate location, or contacts for each subtask.

How to Create a List

It is sometimes easy to get carried away with filling in every little detail into the reminder app, from shopping for groceries to filing tax reports, and so on. Now, you can group all your tasks into lists to make room on your reminder app's home page. Follow the steps below to learn how to achieve this.

- Open the reminders app.
- Navigate to the right bottom of your screen and then click on the "**Add list.**"

- You will see varieties of logos and colors to choose from to help you identify each list at a glance.
- Click on **Done** at the right top side of your screen.
- When you want to add reminders or tasks to this list, go to *My Lists,* to create a new list or move existing tasks to a list.
- For an existing task, open the task, then click on the **"i"** icon to access the options.
- Go down and click on **List** then choose from your new list.

Note: to quickly find a task, you can search using the search bar option.

How to Add a List to a Group

After creating a list and moving tasks to the setlist, you can also bring all the lists in the same category to a general group. Say you have one list for anniversaries and another for birthdays, you can have a group titled "memorable dates" and then move the lists into this group to make your home page look more appealing.

- You can choose to turn off notifications entirely or change the timing for the notification under **Today Notification.**
- You can also modify your tasks' default list while on this screen.

Use Siri as a Reminder

Siri can do a lot of things, which include asking the virtual assistant to remind you of a task. You can say to Siri, "remind me to," followed by the information. If you want Siri to tell you at a specific place or time, ask.

How to Add Siri Shortcuts

With this function, you can quickly assign actions to Siri. Siri now has a more pronounced role in iOS 13, and you have the Siri shortcut app on its own.

- Click on the **Shortcut app** to launch it.
- After which you click on **Create Shortcuts** to create a simple type of shortcut.
- Then click on **Create Shortcuts** to create a simple type of shortcut.
- With the **automation** tab, your device can intelligently react to context as they change. For

instance, you can customize the shortcut to play a particular song each time you get home or design the button to automatically send your location to your partner whenever you are heading home from work.

- In the **Gallery** function, you will find a range of predefined shortcuts to give you some inspiration in designing yours, or you can even make use of the predefined shortcuts.

How to Transfer Content to your iPhone from an Android Phone

You can move contents to your device from an Android mobile phone when you first activate the device or after you did a factory reset. To do this, you will see the **Apps and Data** option on your screen.

- Under **Apps and Data,** click on "**Move Data from Android."**
- You have to install the app "**Move to iOS"** on the android phone before you can move data.
- Click on **Continue** when you have downloaded the app.

- Follow the instructions you see on the screen to move data from the Android to the iPhone.

CHAPTER 2: BASIC FUNCTIONS

How to Wake and Sleep Your iPhone 11

Waking and sleeping your iPhone 11 will preserve your battery life and make it long-lasting; here are the steps to wake and put your iPhone 11 to sleep.

- There are two ways to wake your iPhone 11 and to see the lock screen; either tap the screen or just picking up the device and glancing at it can wake the iPhone 11.

- From the lock screen, you can use either the camera or the flashlight by a simple gesture. Tap and hold the individual icon until you hear a click sound.

- Press the side button to make the iPhone 11 go to sleep. With the Apple Leather Folio case designed for the iPhone 11, open the case to wake and close the case to sleep your device.

How to Turn PIN On or Off

- From **Settings,** click on **Phone.**
- At the bottom of the screen, click on the **SIM PIN.**
- Turn the icon beside SIM PIN to the left or right to put off or on.
- Put in your PIN and click on **Done.** The default PIN for all iPhone 11 is 0000.

How to Change Device PIN

- From **Settings,** click on **Phone.**
- At the bottom of the screen, click on the **SIM PIN.**
- To change the PIN, click on **Change PIN.**
- Type in your current PIN and click **Done.**
- On the next screen, type in the new 4-digit PIN and tap **Done.**
- The next screen will require you to input the PIN again and click on **Done.**

How to Unblock Your PIN

If you enter a wrong PIN 3 consecutive times, it will block the PIN temporarily. Follow the steps to unblock:

- On the home screen, click on **Unlock.**
- Put in the PUK and click on **OK.**

- Click on **Accessibility.**

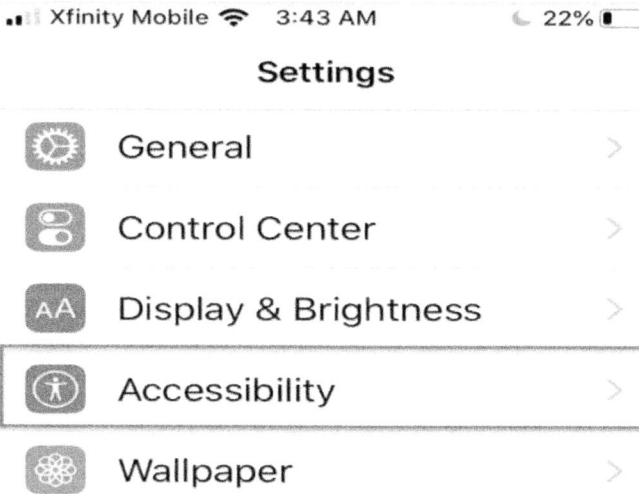

Settings

⚙️ General >

🎛️ Control Center >

AA Display & Brightness >

♿ Accessibility >

✳️ Wallpaper >

- Then click on **3D and Haptic Touch.**

..ıl Xfinity Mobile 🛜 1:01 PM 81% 🔋

< Touch **3D & Haptic Touch**

3D TOUCH

3D Touch ⬤◯

When 3D Touch is on, you can press on
the display to reveal content previews,
actions, and contextual menus.

3D TOUCH SENSITIVITY

Light Medium Firm

Adjust the amount of pressure needed to
activate 3D Touch. Light sensitivity
reduces the amount of pressure required.
Firm sensitivity increases it.

TOUCH DURATION

Fast

Slow ✓

- Disable 3D Touch by moving the slider to the left.
Move the switch to the right to enable the
feature back.

3D TOUCH

3D Touch

When 3D Touch is on, you can press on the display to reveal content previews, actions, and contextual menus.

TOUCH DURATION

Fast

Slow   ✓

How to Enable Dark Mode

At times, the brightness of our phones can be blinding, especially when you pick up your phone in the early hours of the morning due to the bright white theme of your phone. There is now a new **dark mode** feature to help moderate the brightness of your phone. When this feature is active, all your system apps like the iMessage and Safari will be affected. Apple has also called on third-party app developers to design their apps with themes that are compatible with the dark mode. The steps below will show you how to enable the Dark Mode.

- Go to the settings app
- Click on **Display and Brightness**

as the system wallpapers, but they will dim
somewhat when the Dark mode is enabled.

**How to Access Paired Bluetooth Devices from Control
Center**

You can now easily access paired devices on your iPhone
without having to exit a particular app, then navigating
to settings and all the long steps. If you need to pair a
device to Bluetooth, follow the steps below from
anywhere on your phone.

- Go to the control center, make a swipe gesture
  from the right top side of the iPhone down to go
  to the control center.
- You can 3D Touch or click and hold down on the
  wireless connections block at the top right side of
  the screen to expand it.

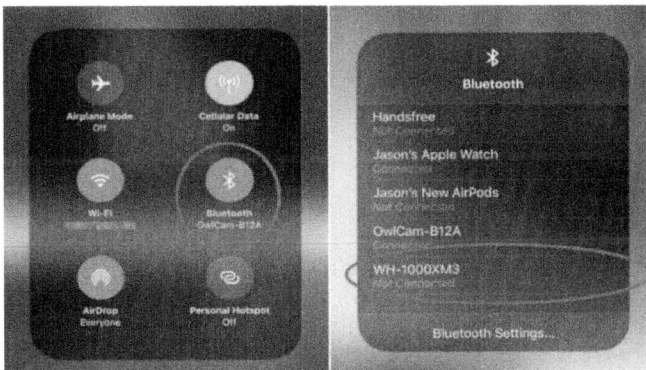

- 3D Touch or Tap and hold the Bluetooth button at the right of the screen.
- On the next screen, you have all the Bluetooth devices, those previously paired, and those available.
- Choose the one you want to connect with.

How to Quickly Connect to Wi-Fi on iOS 13 Through the Control Center

For most of us, we frequently join new Wi-fi networks either when visiting a new location, at the airport or in a restaurant. Now, you have a faster and direct way to connect that does not require launching the settings app. This step will not need you to leave a current app too. Follow the steps below:

- Go to the control center, make a swipe gesture from the right top side of the iPhone down to go to the control center.
- You can 3D Touch, or click and hold down on the wireless connections block at the top right side of the screen to expand it.
- 3D Touch or Tap and hold the Wi-Fi button on the left side of your screen.

- The next screen will display all nearby Wi-fi networks that have been paired previously regardless of their connection status.
- Choose your preferred one to connect.

How to Play Live Radio Through Siri

The iOS 13 brought about some new additions to Siri. You can now get Siri to ply live radio stations by saying, "Hey Siri, "play [name of radio station] radio station." So long as Siri can access the requested radio station, you will hear the station play instantly. Siri has access to over 100,000 radio stations from different parts of the world.

How to Tap and Drag the New Volume Indicator

There is a new volume indicator button that is not as obtrusive as before, and it is something that you can pull up and down. Several people complained that the previous volume indicators were too huge and ate up spaces on the screen. Apple has now replaced it with a small vertical bar placed at the top left of the screen. With your finger, you can drag the bar down and up. As you are dragging the bar, you will see an indicator at the bottom of the bar showing sound output, for example, Bluetooth device, Airpods, or speaker.

How to Control Notification Options

- From Settings, go to **Notifications.**
- Click on **Show Preview** and set to **Always** to be able to preview notification on the lock screen.
- To set this to only when the device is not locked, click on the option "**When Unlocked.**"
- To disable notification preview, select "**Never.**"
- Click on the Back arrow at the top left of the screen.

How to Control Notification for Specific Apps

- From the last step above, Click on the specific application.

- On the next screen, beside **Allow Notifications,** move the slider left or right to enable or disable.

How to Transfer Content to your iPhone 11 from an Android Phone

You can move contents to your device from an Android mobile phone when you first activate the device or after you did a factory reset. To do this, you will see the **Apps and Data** option on your screen.

- Under **Apps and Data,** click on **"Move Data from Android."**
- You have to install the app **"Move to iOS"** on the android phone before you can move data.
- Click on **Continue** when you have downloaded the app.
- Follow the instructions you see on the screen to move data from the Android to the iPhone 11.

How to Control Group Notification

- Scroll down the page and click on **Notification Grouping.**
- Select any of the three options as desired.
- Use the Back button to return.

How to Confirm Software Version

- From **Settings,** go to **General** and click on **About.**

- You will see your device version besides **Version** on the next screen.

How to Update Software

- From **Settings,** go to **General** and click on **Software Update.**

- If there is a new update, it will show on the next screen.

- Then follow the screen instruction to update the software.

How to Control Flight Mode

- From the top right side of the screen, slide downwards.

- Tap the airplane sign representing the flight mode icon to turn off or on.

How to Choose Night Shift Settings

- From **Settings,** go to **Display & Brightness.**

- Click on **Night Shift.**

- To turn off the location service, all you need to do is toggle the button and then select **Turn off** to confirm the action. This will prevent all apps and system services from gaining access to your location data.

How to Use Music Player

- Click on the **Music Player** icon on the home screen.
- Click on **Playlist** then click on **New Playlist.**
- Tap the text box that has **Description,** type in the name for that playlist.
- Click on **Add Music.**
- Go to the category and click on the audio file you want to add.
- Select **Done** at the top of the screen.
- Select **Done** again.
- Go to the playlist and click on the music.
- Use the Volume key to control the volume.
- Click on the song title.
- Tap the right arrow to go to the next music or the left arrow to go to the previous music.
- Gently slide your finger up the screen.

- Click on shuffle to set it on or off.
- Click on **Repeat** to set it on or off. You can choose as many musics as you want to be on **Repeat.**

How to Keep Track of Documents

On your iPhone, you can access folders and files stored on your iCloud Drive and any other cloud storage services. You can also access and restore folders and files deleted from your device within the last 30 days. There are three subsections in the Browse tab, and they are:

1. **Locations:** To view files saved in iCloud, click on **iCloud Drive.** To view files recently deleted from your device, click on **Recently Deleted.**

   To add an external cloud storage service, you need to first install the app from the App Store (Google Drive, Dropbox, etc.), then click **Edit** at the right top corner of your device screen to activate it. Once done, click on **Done.**

   Other available options for folders and files are:

   - To view the content of a folder, click on the folder.

72

- To Copy, Rename, Duplicate, Delete, Move, Tag, Share or Get info of a folder or file, press the folder, or file for some seconds.
- To download items with the cloud and arrow icon, tap on them.
- To annotate a file, click on the pencil tip icon at the right upper side of the screen. It is essential to know that this feature is only available to select image file formats and PDF.

2. **Favorites:** To add folders to the Favorite section, press the folder for some seconds until a menu pops up, then select **Favorite** from the list. Currently, you can only do this from the iCloud Device, and only for folders, no single files.

3. **Tags:** when using macros Finder tags, you will see them in the Tags section. Alternatively, press a file for some seconds to tag such a file. Then click "**A Tag Here**" to see all the files that have that tag.

How to Force Close Apps in the iPhone

You do this mostly when an app isn't responding.

- Merely swiping up from the bottom of the screen will show the app switcher. This will display all the open apps in card-like views.

- For iOS 12 users, to force close the app, locate the app from the app switcher and swipe up to close the app.

- For users still on iOS 11, press the app you wish to close for some seconds until you see the red button marked with the minus sign at the top of each app card.

- Tap on the minus button for each of the apps you wish to close.

- I will advise you upgrade to iOS 12 to enjoy better features on your iPhone.

- To go through apps used in the past, swipe horizontally at the bottom of your home screen.

How to Arrange Home Screen Icons

Follow the steps below to arrange the home screen icon on your iPhone.

Chapter 3: Camera

How to Use Camera

- From the Home screen, tap on Camera
- Move your finger left or right to take you to the **Photo** option, which is after Video by your left and before Portrait by your right.
- Click the flash icon at the top left side of the screen to enable flash
- Then move to the next button after Flash to choose your preferred setting
- Set the camera lens at the back of the device to point at the object you want to capture
- Click on the Take Picture icon, which is the round icon at the bottom of the screen.
- You can draw two fingers apart or together on the screen to either zoom in or out
- Take the picture
- Return to the Home button once done

How to Use Video Recorder

- Click on the Camera icon

- Move your finger left or right to take you to the **Video** option, which is before Photo by your right.
- Tap the Video light icon at the left top of the screen
- Set your desired settings
- Set the camera lens at the back of the device to point at the object you want to capture
- Click on the **Record** icon, which is the round icon at the bottom of the screen.
- You can draw two fingers apart or together on the screen to either zoom in or out
- Tap the **Stop** icon at the bottom of the screen to stop the recording
- Return home once done

How to Send Video Clip or Picture in an MMS

You can send a video clip or picture to another person as an MMS. To do this, follow the listed steps

- Click on Photos
- Go to the desired photo folder
- Click on the desired video clip or picture

- Tap the share button at the left bottom side of the screen with an arrow facing up
- On the next screen, click on **Message**
- On the To field, input the receiver's details
- Click on the Text area to input your message
- Once done, click on the Send button which is the arrow up beside the text box

How to Send Video Clip or Picture in an Email

- Click on Photos
- Go to the desired photo folder
- Click on the desired video clip or picture
- Tap the share button at the left bottom side of the screen with an arrow facing up
- On the next screen, click on **Mail**
- On the To field, input the receiver's details
- Input your email subject on the subject field
- Click on the Text area to input your email message
- Once done, click on **Send** to deliver your email

How to Use Lighting Mode Photo Effects in iOS 13

For pictures captured in portrait mode, your smartphone uses the dual camera to create a depth-of-the-field effect to give you a photo with a blurred background and sharp subject. Now, we have another new feature called the **High-Key Light Mono.** This is similar to the white and black effect of the Stage Light Mono, but you will only get a white background as against a black and white background.

- Go to the photo app and click on a portrait photo.
- To be sure the photo was shot in portrait mode, you will see **"Portrait"** written at the top of the page.
- Then click on **Edit** at the right top corner to go into editing mode.

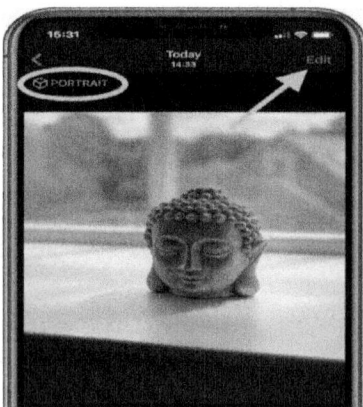

How to Apply Filter to a Video in iOS 13

One new addition that came with iOS 13 is the filter tool. The filter tool is similar to the one you use on Instagram videos.

- From the photo app, choose the video you wish to edit.
- Then click on **Edit at** the right top side of your screen.

- You will see the filter menu at the bottom of the screen (a Venn shape diagram)

- There are nine available filters that you can navigate through for a feel on how each will look on your video.

- Then pick the filter you want and a horizontal dial will appear under that selected filter.

- Slide the dial to adjust the level of intensity of that filter.

- Once you are satisfied with the outcome, click on **Done** at the right bottom side of your screen to affect the filter on your video.

How to Remove Location Details from your Photos

Each time you take photos on your smartphone, the GPS records the exact location the photo was shot. This helps you to view your photos based on location or occasion, especially when sorting out photoshoots. This also means that people who view your pictures on their photo app can see where the place you took the photo. This poses security threats, especially when sharing the images on social media or to a group you have no personal relationship with, as people can trace you home via the location data on the pictures shared. The good news now is that you can remove the location details from your photos before sharing or select persons that should be able to view this information. Apart from photos, you can remove location details from your videos, movies and even multiple images sent via messages, Facebook, Mail, and so on with the steps below:

- After shooting your photos, go to the folder where the picture is stored.
- For a single video or photo, click on the video or photo to open then click on **Share.**
- For multiple videos and pictures, in the section view, click on **Select,** then select all the items for sharing before you click on the **Share** button.
- On the next screen, click on **Options.**

- Move the switch beside **"Location"** to the left to disable this feature.
- Then pick the method you want to use in sending your pictures.

Note: each time you want to share a video or picture, remember to disable location, and the option is only available when sharing the photos or videos directly from your Photo app. Disabling the location feature when sharing does not remove location details from the images and videos saved on your phone.

How to Manually Add or Remove Music and Videos to your iPhone

To manually manage your music and videos, you will have to copy the video files and music tracks to the iPhone from the iTunes Library. Follow the steps below to do this:

- Connect your device to your computer or Mac.
- Launch the iTunes app.
- Manually move the media to the left side of the window.

- Release the media on top of the iPhone (Under Devices).
- Now you can drag any of the items from the main window to the sidebar to add to your iPhone from iTunes.

How to take a Screenshot

Without the home button, taking a snapshot may seem tricky; however, follow these steps to help you make the best shots possible.

- Press both the side and the Volume Up button simultaneously to take a screenshot.
- The photo from the screenshot will be saved automatically in the Photos app, under the **Screenshots** album. Screenshots help you to note down problems you wish to seek help for later.
- To edit the photo, go to the picture and tap the thumbnail at the left bottom corner of your iPhone.
- To view the screenshots in iOS 13, go to **Photos,** then **Albums,** go to **Media Types,** and select **Screenshots.**

CHAPTER 4: Calls and Contacts

How to Answer Call

- Tap any of the volume keys to silence the call notification when a call comes in.
- If the screen lock is active, slide right to answer the call.
- Click on Accept, if there is no screen lock.
- Tap the end call button at the bottom of the screen once done.

How to Call a Number

- Tap the Phone icon on the left.
- Click on Keypads to show the keypads.
- Input the number you want to call then press the call icon.
- Tap the end call button at the bottom of the screen once done.

How to Control Call Waiting

- From **Settings,** click on **Phone** then **Call Waiting.**
- Move the icon beside it to the left or right to enable or disable call waiting.

How to Control Call Announcement

Your device can be set to read out the caller's name when there is an incoming call. The number must be in your address book for this to work.

- From **Settings,** go to **Phone** then **Announce Call.**
- Select **Always** if you want this feature when silent mode is off.
- Choose **Headphones & Car** to activate when your device is connected to a car or a headset.
- The **Headphones Only** option will be for when the device is connected to only headset.
- Select **Never** if you do not wish to turn off this feature.

How to Add Contacts

- At the **Home** screen, select **Extras.**
- Click on **Contacts.**
- Then select the **Add Contact** icon at the right upper side of your screen.
- Enter the details of your contact, including the name, phone number, address, etc.
- Once done with the details, tap **Done,** and your new contact is stored.

How to Merge Similar Contacts

- At the **Home** screen, select **Extras.**

- Click on **Contacts.**

- Click on the contact you want to merge and click on **Edit.**

- At the bottom of the screen, select **Link Contact....**

- Choose the other contact you want to link.

- Click on **Link** at the top right side of the screen.

How to Copy Contact from Social Media and Email Accounts

- From Settings, go to **Accounts and Password.**

- Click on the account, e.g., Gmail.

- Switch on the option beside **Contacts.**

How to Add a Caller to your Contact

- On your call log, click on a phone number.

- You will see options to **Message, Call, Create New Contact, or Add to Existing Contact**.

- Select **Create New Contact.**

- Enter the caller's name and other information you have.

- At the top right hand of the screen, click on **Done.**

How to Add a contact after dialing the number with the keypad

- Manually type in the numbers on the phone app using the number keys.
- Click on the (+) sign on the left side of the number.
- Click on **Create New Contact.**
- Enter the caller's name and other information you have.
- Or click on **Add to Existing Contact.**
- Find the contact name you want to add the contact to and click on the name.
- At the top right hand of the screen, click on **Done.**

How to Import Contacts

The iPhone allows you to import or move your contacts from your phone to the SIM card or SD card for either safekeeping or backup. See the steps below:

- From the Home screen, click on **Settings.**
- Select **Contacts.**
- Chose the option to **"Import SIM Contacts."**

- Chose the account where the contacts should be stored.
- Allow the phone to import the contacts to your preferred account or device.

How to Delete contacts

When you remove unwanted contacts from your device, it makes more space available in your internal memory. Follow the steps below.

- From the Home screen, tap on **Phone** to access the phone app.
- Select **Contacts.**
- Click on the contact you want to remove.
- You will see some options, select **Edit.**
- Move down to the bottom of your screen and click on **Delete Contact.**
- You will see a popup next to confirm your action. Click on **Delete Contact** again.
- The deleted contact will disappear from the available Contacts.

How to Block Spam Calls on iOS 13

A new feature called the "silence unknown callers" was added to iOS 13. You can now block spam calls without having to block each one individually. With this method, the caller is not permanently barred as their calls are sent straight to voicemail, and should you discover that a blocked call is not spam, you can go to your voicemail to listen to the message and call back whoever you need to contact. The steps below will show you how to enable the new call blocker:

- From the settings app, click on **Phone.**
- Navigate to *Silence Unknown Callers* and move the switch to the right to enable it.

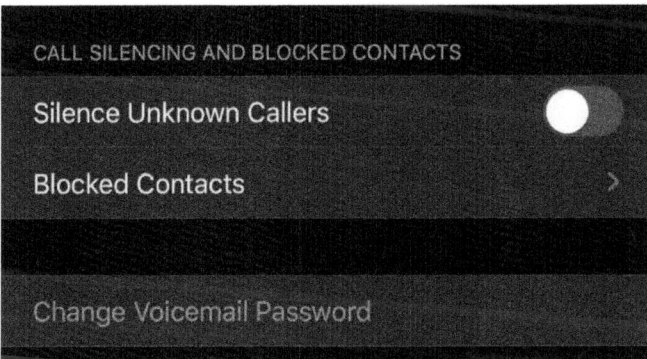

CALL SILENCING AND BLOCKED CONTACTS

Silence Unknown Callers

Blocked Contacts

Change Voicemail Password

This feature will automatically send unknown callers to voicemails and will give you less to worry about robocalls and spam calls.

How to Block Spam, Contacts and Unknown Senders

Any email received from blocked senders will be sent straight to the trash folder. Like the "silence unknown callers" feature, you are not blocking the senders as you can always go to the trash folder to see messages sent in there, which is better than preventing the contacts totally from reaching you. At the moment, Apple has a single folder where you will see all blocked spammers and contacts. So, for all the phone numbers you may have blocked in the past either from the Messages app, FaceTime, or Phone, you can find them together with the blocked email addresses. You will first have to complete your block settings. This setting is what determines what the mail app should do with emails received from blocked contacts.

- From the settings app, click on **Mail.**
- Then go to **Threading.**

- Click on **Blocked Sender,** and you will see three options

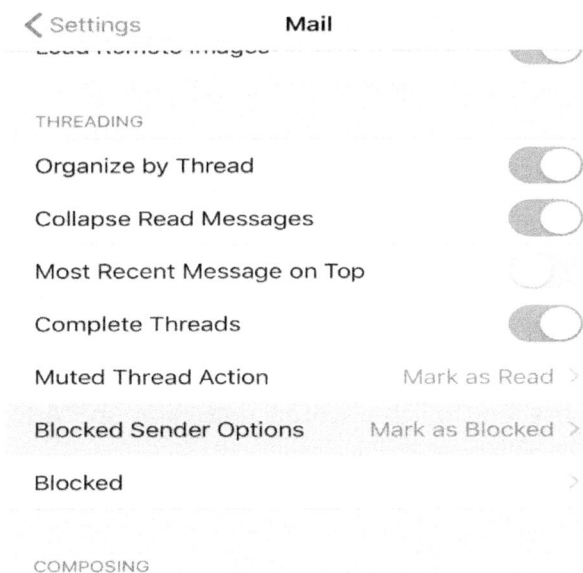

‹ Settings   **Mail**

THREADING

Organize by Thread

Collapse Read Messages

Most Recent Message on Top

Complete Threads

Muted Thread Action   Mark as Read ›

Blocked Sender Options   Mark as Blocked ›

Blocked   ›

COMPOSING

- If you enable the option for **None,** it will automatically disable the email blocking feature.

- The option, "**Mark as Blocked, Leave in Inbox,**" means that you will receive emails from your blocked contacts directly in your inbox without being notified.

- The option, "**Move to Trash,**" will send all emails from blocked contacts to the trash folder. You can choose to set the trash folder to delete automatically, or to delete it manually.

95

Note: this feature will apply to all the accounts you have in your mail app, including Outlook, Gmail, Yahoo, etc.

Block a Contact Via Settings App

Another way to block a sender is via the settings app.

- Go to the settings app and click on **Mail.**
- Go down on the page then click on **Blocked.**
- On this screen, you will see all the blocked email addresses and phone numbers.
- Go to the end of the screen and click on **"Add New."**
- You will receive a prompt to choose the select to block.
- The number or email address will immediately appear on the blocked list.

Note: you need to have saved the contact of the person you wish to block to be able to use this option. If you do not have the email address saved, then you may have to block them from the inbox.

How to Block a Contact Through Their Received Emails

Whenever you receive an email from an unknown sender or someone you do not wish to read from again, you can get them blocked right in that email.

- Click on the contact fields at the top of the email to see all the parties in the send list.
- Then click on the email address you want to block.
- On the next screen, you will see an expanded menu option.
- Click on **Block this contact,** then click on the prompt again to accept your action.
- And that email address is blocked!
- Every message received from that email address, whether in the present or past, will have a blocked hand icon close to the date in the header for email. Every email from a blocked contact will also have a notification at the top that says **"This message is from a sender in your blocked list."**

How to Unblock a Sender Through Received Email

For blocked email addresses, you can unblock by going to the sender's contact details in the email and then click on "Unblock this Contact." The hand icon may not instantly disappear, but the sender will be unblocked immediately.

How to Unblock a Contact

The settings app brings together the list of blocked contacts, and so, from the same way, you can unblock a contact through the settings app.

- Use the steps above to access the list of blocked contacts.
- Then short swipe from the left side of the email address or phone number you want to unblock.
- After which, you click on **Unblock.**
- Alternatively, you can make a long swipe on the contact to unblock it automatically.
- Another way is to click on **Edit** at the right top of your screen, then click on the "-"minus button beside the email address or phone number you want to unblock, then click on **Unblock.**

How to Use and Manage Call Forwarding on your iPhone

With the Call Forwarding Unconditional (CFU) feature in the iPhone, calls will go straight to a separate phone number without the main device ringing. This is most useful when you do not wish to turn off ringer or disregard a call but also do not want to be distracted by such calls. To enable this feature, follow the steps below:

- Go to **Settings** from Home.
- Click on **Phone** then **Call Forwarding.**
- Select the **Forward to** option.
- Input the second number where you want to receive the calls. It could be your voicemail.

Apart from CFU, Call Forwarding Conditional (CFC) allows you to forward incoming calls to a different number if the call goes unanswered on your number. To enable this feature, you need to have the shortcodes for call forwarding then set the options to your preference. For these shortcodes, reach out to your carrier.

How to Cancel Call Forwarding on your iPhone

To cancel,

- Go to **Settings** then **Phone**
- Click on **Call Forwarding.**
- Move the slider to switch off the feature.

How to Set Do Not Disturb

Your device can be in silent mode for a defined period. Even though your phone is in silent mode, you can set to receive notification from particular callers.

- Under **Settings,** click on **Do Not Disturb.**
- Toggle the switch next to **"Do Not Disturb"** to the right to enable this function.
- Toggle the switch next to **"Scheduled"** to the right. Then, follow instructions on your screen to set the period for the DND.
- Under **Silence**, select **"Always"** if you want your device to be permanently on silent mode.
- Select **"While iPhone is locked"** if you want to limit this to only when the phone is locked.
- Scroll down and click on **"Allow Calls from."**
- Chose the best setting that meets your need to set the contacts that can reach you while on DND.

- Click on the back arrow at the top left of the screen.
- Scroll down to **Repeated Calls** and switch the button on or off as needed.
- Click on **"Activate"** under **"Do Not Disturb While Driving."**
- On the next screen, choose your preferred option.
- Click on the back button to return to the previous screen.
- Scroll down and select **"Auto Reply-To".**
- On the next screen, select the contacts you wish to notify that **Do Not Disturb While Driving** is on.
- Go back to the previous screen.
- Scroll down and select **Auto Reply,** then follow the instructions on the screen to set your auto-response message.

CHAPTER 5: Messages and Emails

How to Set up your Device for iMessaging

- From Settings, go to Messages.
- Enable iMessages by moving the slider to the right.

How to Set up Your Device for MMS

- From **Settings**, go to **Messages**.
- Enable **MMS Messaging** by moving the slider to the right.

How to Compose and Send iMessage

- From the Message icon, click on the new message option at the top right of the screen.
- Under the "To" field, type in the first few letters of the receiver's name.
- Select the receiver from the drop-down.
- You will see iMessage in the composition box only if the receiver can receive iMessage.
- Click on the "Text Input Field" and type in your message.
- Click on the send button beside the composed message.

- You will be able to send video clips, pictures, audios, and other effects in your iMessage.

How to Compose and Send SMS

- From the Message icon, click on the new message option at the top right of the screen.
- Under the "To" field, type in the first few letters of the receiver's name.
- Select the receiver from the drop-down.
- Click on the "Text Input Field" and type in your message.
- Click on the send button beside the composed message.

How to Compose and Send SMS with Pictures

- From the Message icon, click on the new message option at the top right of the screen.
- Under the "To" field, type in the first few letters of the receiver's name.
- Select the receiver from the drop-down.
- Click on the "Text Input Field" and type in your message.
- Click the Camera icon on the left side of the composed message.

- From Photos, go to the right folder.
- Select the picture you want to send.
- Click **Choose** and then **Send.**

How to Hide Alerts in Message app on your iPhone

- Go to the **Message app** on your iPhone.
- Open the conversation you wish to hide the alert.
- Click on the **(i)** button at the upper right corner of the page.
- Among the options, one of them is '**Hide alerts**', move the switch to the right to turn on the option (the switch becomes green).
- Select '**Done**' at the right upper corner of your screen. You are good to go!

How to Set a Profile Picture and Name in iMessages

Setting a profile picture and name in iMessages saves users from first saving your contact details to decipher who sent a message. You can choose who you will like to be able to access this feature. Follow the steps below to set this up.

- Open the messages app.

- Click on the three dots (...) at the right upper corner of your screen.

- Then click on **Edit Name and Photo.**

- Select a profile picture and type in your last and first names.

- You can either create your own Memoji to use as your profile picture or select from available Animoji.

- On the next screen, you can choose the settings for sharing this detail from any of the following options: with *Anyone, Contacts Only,* or to *Always Ask* if the details are to be shared.

How to Specify View for your Profile Picture and Name in iMessages

You can choose who you will like to be able to view your profile picture and name. This setting is used to limit users who can access your details.

- From the settings from **Share Automatically,** you have three options to choose from regarding sharing your name and profile picture.

- Use the **Contacts Only** option to share details with only persons whose numbers you have saved on your smartphone.
- **Anyone** option gives access to everyone that has your contact details.
- If you want the system always to prompt you to choose who to share with, then click on the **Always Ask** option. Whenever you open a new incoming message, you will see a pop up on your screen asking for permission to share details with the sender. To share your details, click on **Share** if otherwise, click on "**X**" to refuse and shut down the message.

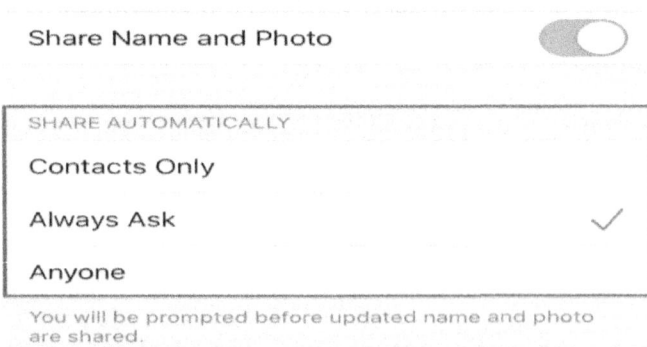

Share Name and Photo

SHARE AUTOMATICALLY

Contacts Only

Always Ask

Anyone

You will be prompted before updated name and photo are shared.

How to Create and Use Animoji or Memoji

The steps below will show you how to create a cartoon version of yourself or your loved ones.

- From the settings for name and profile picture, click on the circle for photos close to the name field.
- Then click on the "+" sign to design your own Memoji.

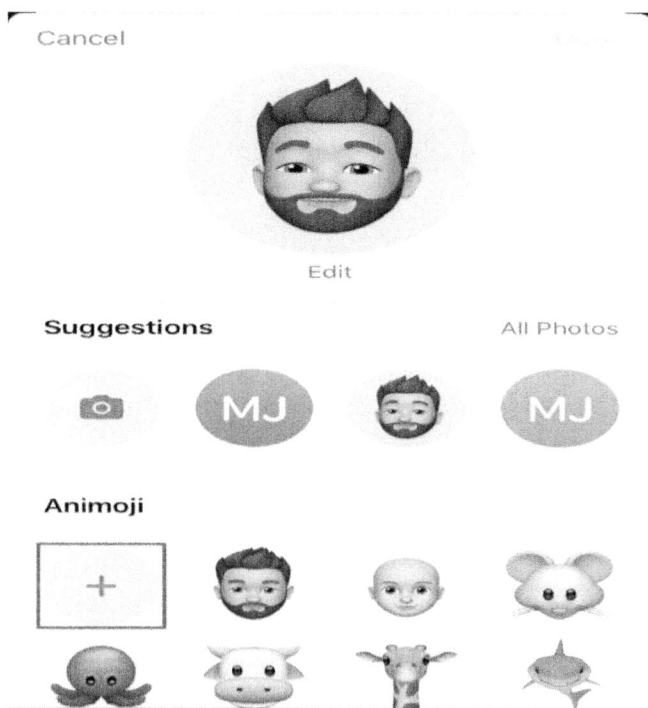

Cancel

Edit

Suggestions   All Photos

MJ   MJ

Animoji

+

- After you must have created one, click on it to choose a pose for your Memoji and to also use it as your profile picture.

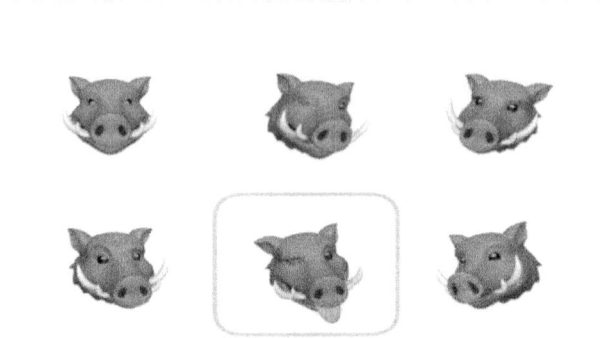

- If you prefer to use a non-personal image, you can select from available Animoji. The Animoji menu selection has several options including sharks and mouse.
- After you must have selected an Animoji or Memoji, scale it, then fit it into the circle.
- Choose a background color to complete your setup.

How to Customize Your Memoji and Animoji

You can create your own Memoji and Animoji through the steps below:

- Go to iMessage.

- Click on a conversation to launch it.

- Click on the Memoji icon.

- Then click on the "+" button.

How to Create New Contacts from Messages On iPhone

- Go to the Messages app.

- Click on the conversation with the sender whose contact you want to add.

- Above the conversation, you will see their phone number.

- Click on the phone number.

- This will show three buttons on the screen.

- Click on the **Info** option.

- You will see the number again at the top of the screen, click on it.

- Then click **Create New Contact**.

- Input their name and other details you have on them.

- At the top right hand of the screen, click on **Done**.

How to Set up Your Device for POP3 Email

- From Settings, go to **Accounts and Password**.

- Click on **Add account.**
- Select your service provider from the list or click on others If your service provider is not on the list.
- Select **Add Mail Account.**
- Input your details, name, email address, and password.
- Under Description, put in your desired name.
- Click on **Next** at the top right corner of the page.
- The next screen is a confirmation that your email has been set up.
- Follow the on-screen instructions to enter any extra information.

How to Set up Your Device for IMAP Email

- From Settings, go to **Accounts and Password.**
- Click on **Add account.**
- Select your service provider from the list or click on others If your service provider is not on the list.
- Select **Add Mail Account.**

- Input your details, name, email address, and password.
- Under Description, put in your desired name.
- Click on **Next** at the top right corner of the page.
- The next screen is a confirmation that your email has been set up.
- Follow the on-screen instructions to enter any extra information.
- After this, select **IMAP,**
- Under hostname, type in the name of your email provider's incoming server.
- Fill in the username and password for your account.
- Under outgoing host server, type in the name of your email provider's outgoing server.
- Click **Next.**
- Select "**Save**" at the top right of the screen to save your email address.

How to Set up Your Device for Exchange Email

- From Settings, go to **Accounts and Password.**
- Click on **Add account.**

- Select **Exchange** under email service provider.
- Input your email address.
- Under Description, put in your desired name.
- Click on **Sign In.**
- Input your email password on the next screen.
- Click on **Sign In.**
- Move the indicator next to the needed data type to enable or disable data synchronization.
- Select **Save** at the top right of the screen to save your email address.

How to Delete Email Account

- From Settings, go to **Accounts and Password.**
- Click on the email address you want to delete.
- Select **Delete Account** at the bottom of the page.
- On the next screen, click on **Delete from my iPhone.**

How to Compose and Send Email

- From the Home screen, select the Mail icon.
- Click on the back arrow at the top left of the screen.
- Select the sending email address.

- Click the new email icon at the bottom right side of the screen.
- On the To field, input the receiver email address and the subject of the email.
- Write your email content in the body of the email.
- To insert a video or picture, press and hold the text input field until a pop-up menu comes up on the screen.
- Click **Insert Pictures or Videos** from the pop-up and then follow the instructions you see on the screen to attach the media.
- To attach a document, select **"Add Attachment"** and follow the instructions you see on the screen.
- Click on **Send** at the right top of the screen.

How to Use Swipe Typing

The swipe typing feature is now a default feature in the iPhone keyboard. With this feature, you can type on your screen with a swipe of your fingers across the keys of your keyboard instead of clicking on each word. The keyword will deduce the right words you are entering and then insert it into your message. It may seem confusing at the first use, but once you get familiar with it, you will realize that you type faster with this than when you are tapping on each key. By default, the feature is enabled on your device, and it does not require any further action to be able to use it. For instance, if you want to type "friend," tap on the "f" key on your keyboard then swipe your finger over the "r," "I," up till "d" keys in the correct order. The keyboard will automatically pick up the words you wish to type. This method is faster than manually tapping on different keys. One downside, though, is that swipe typing may not be as accurate as the regular typing, but this can be corrected. Each time you finish swiping, you will see three options on your keyboard for the words swiped, and you can click on the right one. If the keyboard entered the right word, rather than clicking, you can continue to swipe your next words for the system to automatically select it. The keyboard has been designed to get better the more you make use of the feature, but when dealing with uncommon words, it is advisable to begin by tap typing first.

How to Disable Swipe Typing

If you find this feature hard to use or annoying, you can use the steps below to disable it.

- Go to the settings app.
- Click on **General.**
- Then select **Keyboards.**
- Navigate to **"Slide to Type"** and move the switch to the left to disable the option.

Text Replacement	>
One Handed Keyboard	Off >

Auto-Capitalization

Auto-Correction

Check Spelling

Enable Caps Lock

Predictive

Smart Punctuation

Delete Slide-to-Type by Word

Slide to Type

Character Preview

"." Shortcut

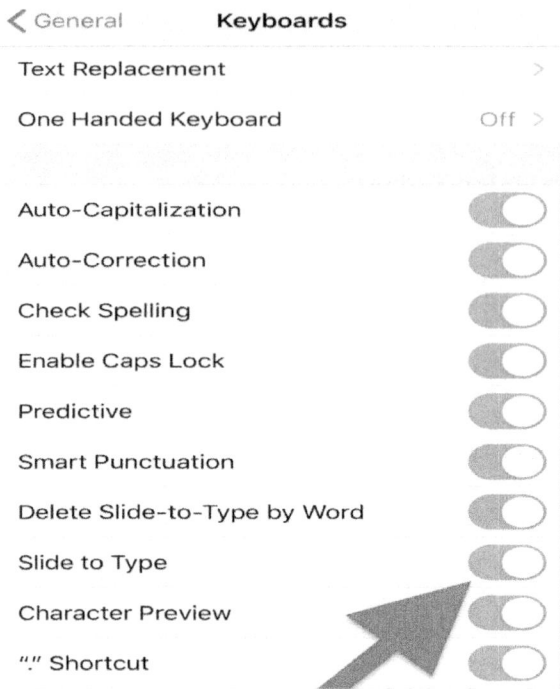

You can also disable the feature using the keyboard.

- Long press on the keyboard switcher.

- Then click on **Keyboard settings.**

- Depending on your keyboard setup, you will see the switcher as a Globe icon or an Emoji icon.

- Navigate to **"Slide to Type"** and move the switch to the left to disable the option.

Note: To disable with the keyboard method, you need to have more than one keyboard activated on your device.

How to Use the New Gestures for Copy, Cut, Paste, Redo and Undo

For most of us, we use the iPhone as our primary way of communicating with people as well as performing other functions, and for this reason, it is more productive to know how to manage the text features outside the "shake to undo" gesture in the old iOS. While the "shake to undo" gesture is still available, Apple has now added a 3-finger gesture to make it easy for typing.

How to Copy, Cut and Paste

To get the best results on this feature, I will advise that you use your two fingers and thumb, which can be quite tricky if performing this on a small screen.

- To copy, use your three fingers to pinch on the text and then un-pinch (expand your fingers) using your three fingers to Paste the text you copied.
- Perform the copy gesture twice with your finger to cut out the text. While the first gesture will copy the text, the second gesture will cut out the text.

- If you look at the top of your screen, you will see the badges for "Copy," "Cut," or "Paste" to verify your action.

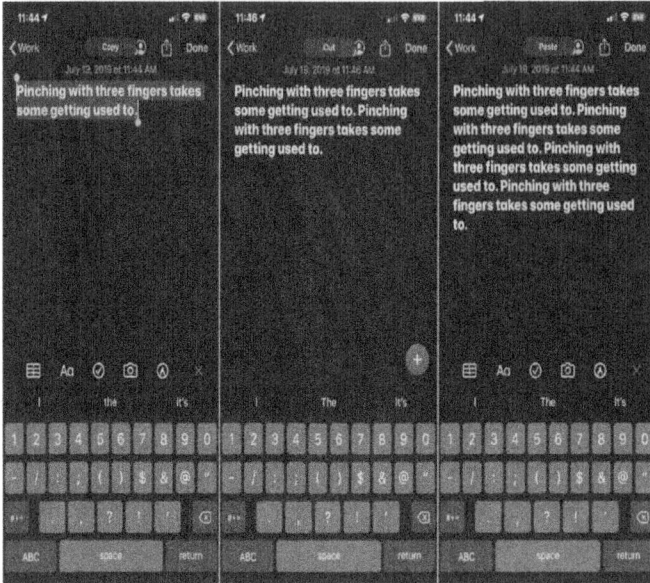

How to Redo and Undo

- To undo, swipe to the left with your three fingers on the screen.

- Another way to undo is by double-clicking on the screen with your three fingers.

- To Redo, swipe to the right with your three fingers on the screen.

- If you look at the top of your screen, you will see the badges for "Redo" or "Undo" to verify your action.

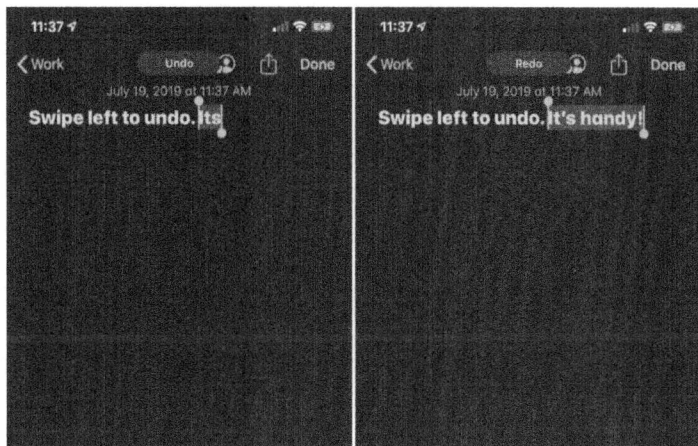

CHAPTER 6: Manage Applications and Data

How to Install Apps from the App Store

- Open the app store and click on search.

- Type the name of the app into the search field.

- Click on **Search.**

- Select the desired app.

- Click on **GET** beside the app and follow the steps on the screen to install the app. For paid apps, click on the price to install.

How to Uninstall an App

To uninstall an app,

- Click and hold the app until it begins to shake.

- Click on the **Delete** option, then select **Delete.**

With this method, every setting and data about the app will delete from your phone.

How to Delete Apps in iOS 13

The steps below will show you how to delete apps fast.

- When you long-press on an app on your home screen, it will show option to rearrange the apps.

- Click on the displayed option to set the apps to wiggle mode, and you will see an **X mark** beside each app icon.
- Go to the app you wish to delete and click on the **X** icon.

You also have the option to delete apps from the App store. When viewing or updating apps in the app store, you can make a swipe gesture to the left on any app you want to delete to see the option for **Delete.** This is a convenient way to remove apps from within the app store. Permit me to explain the steps in detail.

- Go to the app store.
- You will see your account picture at the right top corner of your screen, click on it.
- Go to the section for **Updated Recently**
- If you wish to delete any recently updated app, make a swipe gesture to the left on the particular app you want to remove.
- Then click on the red button that will appear on your screen.

How to Delete Apps from the Update Screen

This is yet another way to delete apps you no longer want.

- From the app store, you will notice that the update for apps is now under the **Account card.** (click on your picture at the right top of your screen)
- If you see any app you wish to delete from the displayed list, make a swipe gesture to the left on that particular app, and you will see the option to delete the app.
- You can use this step for all the apps you see in the list whether the app has been updated or is pending update.

How to Delete Apps Without Losing the App Data

- From the **Settings,** go to **General.**
- Click **iPhone Storage.**
- Click on the app you wish to uninstall and click on **Offload App.**
- Select **Offload App** again to complete.

How to Control Automatic App Update

- From the **Settings,** go to **iTunes and App Store.**

- Besides the **"Update" option,** move the switch left or right to control it.
- Move to **"Use Mobile Data,"** move the switch left or right to enable or disable.

How to Choose Settings for Background Refresh of Apps

- From the **Settings,** go to **General.**
- Click on **Background App Refresh.**
- Then click on **Background App Refresh** again.
- Select **OFF** to disable.
- To refresh the apps using Wi-fi, select **Wi-fi.**
- Select **Wi-fi and Mobile Data** if you want to be able to refresh using mobile data.
- Use the back button to return to the previous screen.
- For each of the apps listed, move the slide either left or right to enable or disable.

How to configure your iPhone for manual syncing

- Using either Wi-fi or USB, connect your device to a computer.
- Manually open the iTunes app if it doesn't come up automatically.

- Tap on the iPhone icon on the top- left of the iTunes screen. If you have multiple iDevices, rather than seeing the iPhone icon, you will see menu showing all the connected iDevices. Once the devices are displayed, select your current device.
- Tap on the **Apply** button at the bottom right corner of your screen.
- Tap on the Sync button if it doesn't start syncing automatically.

How to Sign in to iCloud on your iPhone.

- Go to the **Settings app.**
- At the top of your screen, click on **Sign in to your iPhone.**

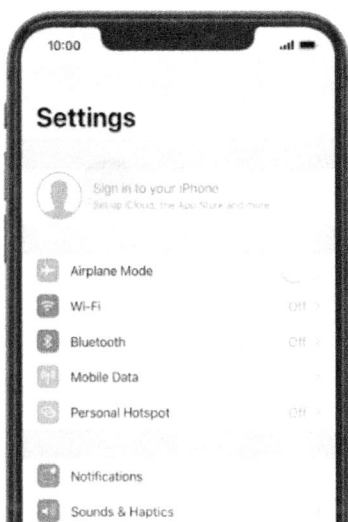

- Enter your Apple ID email address and password.

- Then click on **Sign In.**

- The next screen will ask for your device passcode if you set up one.

- Set the iCloud Photos the way up like them.

- Switch **Apps using iCloud** on or off, however you want it.

How to Sign Out of iCloud on Your iPhone

- From the **Settings app,** click on **Apple ID.**

- Click on **Sign Out** at the bottom of the screen.

- Input your Apple ID password then select **Turn Off.**

- Chose the data you will like to keep a copy of on your iPhone and move the switch on.

- At the top right corner of your screen, click on **Sign Out**.

- Click on **Sign Out** to confirm your decision.

How to Use iCloud Backup

To use the iCloud backup, ensure that your device is connected to Wi-fi before you proceed. To back up, follow the steps below

- Navigate to **Settings>Name>iCloud.** If you are using other iOS, go to **Settings>iCloud.**

- Look out for the button titled **'Backup" or "iCloud Backup,"** switch it on.

- Connect your smartphone to Wi-fi and ensure to connect to a working charge point during the process.

- Once done with the backup, visit **Settings>Name>iCloud>iCloud Storage>Manage Storage** to confirm the phone backup.

How to share a calendar on iPhone via iCloud

To share your calendar on your iPhone, it is essential to first of all turn on the iCloud for calendar option. Kindly follow the steps below:

- On your iPhone, go to **'settings.'**
- Click on your device name and select **"iCloud."**
- Then turn on **"Calendars."**

After you must have done this, you can now share your calendar by following these steps:

- Open the **"Calendar"** app on your device.
- At the bottom of your screen, select **"calendars."**
- You will see an **"info"** icon next to the calendar you want to share, click on the icon.
1. Select the **'add person"** option on the screen then pick the people you wish to share the calendar with.
2. Tap "add" followed by "Done" at the top of your screen.

How to Synchronize using iCloud

- Click on your Apple ID under Settings.
- Click on iCloud.

- Scroll down to **iCloud Drive** and move the switch left or right to enable or disable.
- Under iCloud, click on **Photos.**
- Scroll down to **Upload to My Photo Stream** and slide left to right to activate or disable.

How to Troubleshoot if iCloud isn't Working

If your iCloud isn't working, follow the steps below:

- Ensure the Wi-fi is connected and strong as this is usually the main reason if iCloud backup does not respond.

- Once done, confirm that you have sufficient space in the cloud. Apple gives you only 5G free. If you have used up the free space, clear the files you don't need or instead back them up with iTunes then remove them from the iCloud backup.

- If you do not wish to delete any information, the next step will be to purchase additional room in the iCloud. The pricing is shown below:

50 GB per month: 0.99 USD

200GB per month: 2.99 USD

2 TB per month: 9.99 USD

- Finally, remove any irrelevant data from the iPhone or computer before you perform the iCloud backup.

How to Choose Settings for Find my iPhone

- Click on your Apple ID under Settings.
- Click on iCloud.
- Scroll down and click on **Find My iPhone**.
- Slide left to right to activate or disable.
- Scroll down to **"Send Last Location"** and Slide left to right to activate or disable.

How to Use the Look Around Feature in Apple Maps

If you are familiar with the Streetview from Google, you can relate to Apple's Look Around Feature. This feature allows you to preview a particular location before you physically visit. The steps below will guide you on how to use this feature.

- Type your desired location in the Apple Map's search bar.

- Then press long on the map to select this location.

- Every location that supports the Look Around feature will show a **look around** image on the screen.

- Click on the **Look Around** image to go to the street level and then drag to look around the location.

- This screen also shows you facts about the location, and you can swipe up from the bottom of your screen to add the area to your favorites list.

While you may not be able to use this for all the locations in the USA yet, however, Apple has promised that they will cover the whole of USA by the end of 2019 after which they will follow suit for other countries.

How to Use Favorites in the Apple Maps

There has always been an Apple map, but it had limited features. Now, the iOS 13 brought several improvements to Apple map which includes beaches, roads, buildings, and other exciting details. Some other cool features were added recently, like being able to add a location to your list of Favorites. Another exciting feature is the ability to organize all your saved places in a personal customized collection. Follow the steps below to add a favorite on the map.

- Manually search for a location by inputting the address or click on the desired location.
- Navigate to the bottom of your screen and click on **Add to Favorites.**
- Whenever you want to view your favorites list, go to your main page on the Apple map app.

To begin a new collection,

- Go to the main page for the Apple map.
- Swipe from the bottom of the screen upwards.
- Then click on **New Collections** to make a new list.

To add a particular location to your customized collection,

- Drag up from the Apple maps' main page and click on **My Places.**
- Select **Add a Place.**
- On the next screen, add all your recently viewed location to your collection or use the search bar to find a particular area and add to the group.

How to Pair your iPhone with an Xbox One S controller

- From the settings app, click on **Bluetooth** to enable the Bluetooth menu.

- The **Xbox One** controller has to be 100% charged.

- Press the Xbox logo button to power it on.

- Go to the back of the controller and press the wireless enrollment button there. Hold down the button for some seconds.

- Please skip this step if you have already unpaired the controller from a different device. You can press and hold the Xbox button to put it in pairing mode.

- If you haven't unpaired before, continue with the steps below.

- The Xbox button light will begin to flash quickly.

- Go to your Bluetooth menu on your smartphone and locate the "Xbox Wireless Controller" from the list, then click on it.

- Once the light stops blinking and remains focused, then you know that pairing is complete.

How to Disconnect Xbox One Controller from your iPhone

To disconnect using the controller, hold down the Xbox button for approximately 10 seconds. If you will rather disconnect via the iPhone, it is best to go through the control center.

- For Face ID compatible iPhones, go to the control center by swiping diagonally from the top right to the lower left of your screen.
- For Touch ID compatible iPhone, with your finger, swipe from the bottom up.
- Hold down the Bluetooth icon on your screen.
- When you see a pop-up menu on your screen, press down on *Bluetooth: On.*
- Then on the next pop up, you will see the name "Xbox Wireless Controller" showing on the list.
- Click on the controller to completely disconnect from your device.

You can also go through another step shown below:

- From the settings app, click on **Bluetooth.**
- From the pop-up on your screen, press down on *Bluetooth: On.*

- Then on the next pop up, you will see the name "Xbox Wireless Controller." showing on the list.
- Click on the controller to completely disconnect from your device.

There is yet another method, as shown below:

- From the settings app, click on **Bluetooth.**
- Then go to the list for **My Devices,** you will find "Xbox Wireless Controller."
- Besides the controller option to the right, you will see an "I" icon in a blue circle. Click on the icon.
- From the next pop-up, click on **Disconnect.**
- Just press the Xbox button when next you want to use the controller on your iPhone.

How to Unpair the Xbox Controller from your iPhone

Follow the steps on disconnecting the devices but rather than clicking on **Disconnect,** click on **"Forget This Device"**

How to Pair your iPhone with a DualShock 4

You can now take your gaming experience to the next level by playing games on your iPhone with the

DualShock 4. The steps below will show you how to pair the controller with your iPhone.

- From the settings app, click on **Bluetooth** to enable the Bluetooth menu.
- The DualShock 4 controller should be fully charged.
- Press both the Share and PlayStation Button of the controller at the same time and hold down for a few seconds.
- You should see lights begin to flash intermittently at the back of the controller.
- Go to the Bluetooth menu on your iPhone, and you will find the DualShock 4 Wireless controller as one of the devices on the displayed list.
- Click on the controller.
- Once the blinking light at the back of the controller changes to reddish-pink color, it means that the devices have paired.

How to Disconnect a DualShock 4 from your iPhone

Whenever you are not making use of the controller, I will advise you to turn off the Bluetooth connection. If you rather go through the controller, hold down the PlayStation button for approximately 10 seconds. You can also use the steps below to disconnect directly on your iPhone.

- For Face ID compatible iPhones, go to the control center by swiping diagonally from the top right to the lower left of your screen.
- For Touch ID compatible iPhone, with your finger, swipe from the bottom up.
- Hold down the Bluetooth icon on your screen.
- When you see a pop-up menu on your screen, press down on *Bluetooth: On.*
- Then on the next pop up, you will see the name "DUALSHOCK 4 Wireless Controller" showing on the list.
- Click on the controller to completely disconnect from your device.

You can also go through another step shown below:

- From the settings app, click on **Bluetooth.**
- From the pop-up on your screen, press down on *Bluetooth: On.*

- Then on the next pop up, you will see the name "DUALSHOCK 4 Wireless Controller" showing on the list.
- Click on the controller to completely disconnect from your device.

There is yet another method, as shown below:

- From the settings app, click on **Bluetooth.**
- Then go to the list for **My Devices,** you will find "DUALSHOCK 4 Wireless Controller."
- Besides the controller option to the right, you will see an "I" icon in a blue circle. Click on the icon.
- From the next pop-up, click on **Disconnect.**

After the first successful pairing of the controller to your iPhone, when next you want to play with the controller, you need to press the PlayStation button with Bluetooth enabled on your iPhone for both devices to pair.

How to Unpair the DualShock 4 from your iPhone

After you must have disconnected the controller from your iPhone, it does not unpair both devices. The PlayStation may accidentally connect to the iPhone when stuffed in a bag or enclosed position. Because of cases like this, it is advisable to unpair both devices and then follow the steps to re-pair then on your next use. Follow the steps on disconnecting the devices but rather than clicking on **Disconnect,** click on **"Forget This Device"** instead.

How to Download Large Apps over Cellular Network

Before now, the system will require that you connect to Wi-fi before downloading large apps. Now, when downloading apps above 200MB, you will see a pop up to confirm if you will want to continue the download using your cellular data, or, you will download it **"Later on Wi-Fi."** But you need to first enable this feature from settings.

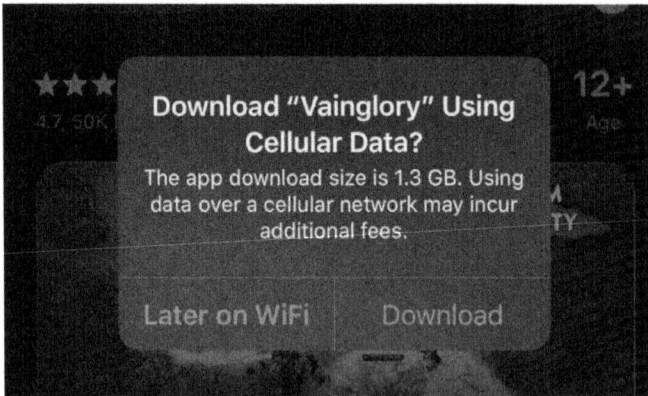

- From the settings app, click on the **iTunes & App Store.**

- On the next screen, there are three options to choose from: one is to allow you download your apps over cellular, second is always to ask if you want to continue on cellular, and the third is to ask you only when the app is over 200MB.

How to Scan Documents Straight to Files App

Your phone has an in-built scanner that you can use for scanning your documents and save them as PDF. You also have the option of choosing where the scanned files should be stored. This is one of the new supports from the iOS 13 upgrade. Follow the steps below to use this feature.

- Go to the Files app.

- From any location in the app, pull down a little to display the options for **View** (View and Sorting style).

- Click on the 3-dot (…) icon at the left side of your screen to see the 3 available options: "Scan Documents," "New Folder," and "Connect to Server."

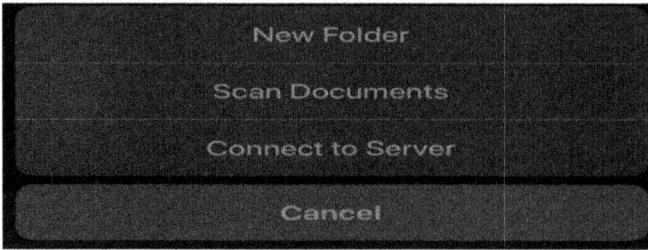

- Click on **Scan Documents** and scan your receipts or forms into PDF format and have it saved in any of your preferred cloud folders.

How to Save Screenshots in the Files App on Your iPhone

If you want, you can choose to save your screenshots in the Files app instead of the Photos app. The steps below will show you how to achieve this.

- After taking your screenshot, click on the little preview in the Markup to edit it.
- Click on **Done.**
- You will notice that a new option which is the **"Save to Files."**
- Click on **Save to Files** to save the screenshots in your network folders or iCloud or other Files location outside the Photos app.

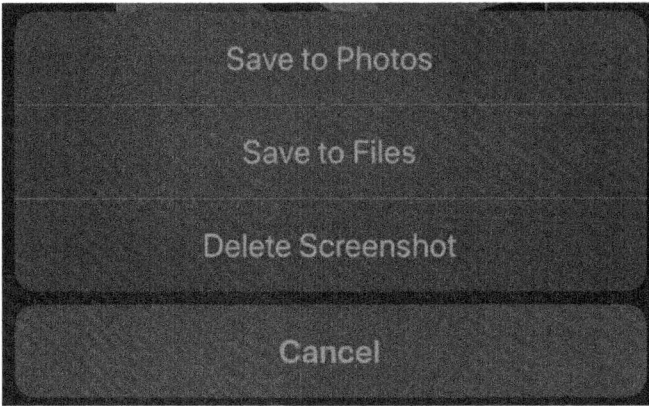

Save to Photos

Save to Files

Delete Screenshot

Cancel

CHAPTER 7: Internet and Data

How to Access Website Settings for Safari

The Safari browser witnessed several additions and upgrades with the iOS 13. One of these changes is the ability to customize different settings for different websites. Similar to how it works on the Safari browser for your Mac device, you are now able to modify security and viewing options differently for each website settings. Safari then applies the settings so that you do not have to run them repeatedly. The steps below will show you how to achieve this.

- Visit a site that you use regularly.
- Tap on the "aA" icon at the left top corner of your screen to show the **View menu** of the website.
- Select **Website settings.**

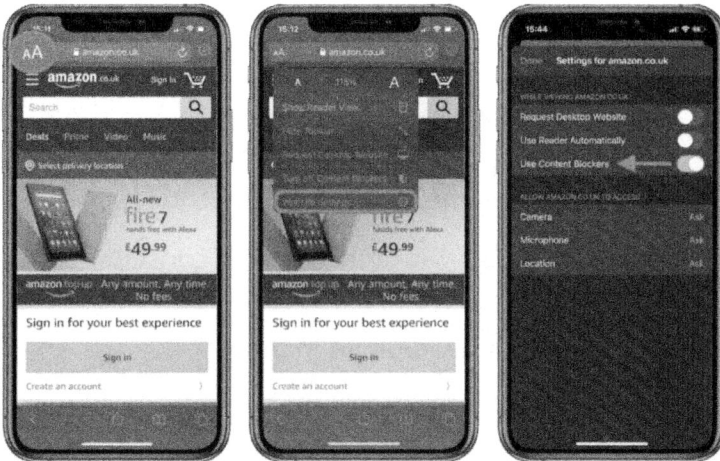

- You will see three options displayed, as shown below:

➤ **Request Desktop Website:** click on this to view original desktop versions of a website on your mobile device.

➤ **Reader Mode** option helps to make online articles more readable by removing extraneous web page contents from it. You can enable this icon by clicking on **"Use Reader Automatically"** to activate this feature by default.

➤ **Camera, Microphone, Location:** these last three options allow you to choose if you want sites to have access to your device microphone, camera as well as if the sites should be able to know your location. You can choose either **Deny** or **Allow,** but if you want to have different options per time, then you should select the option for **Ask.** This way, whenever sites wish to access these features, Safari will first seek your consent.

How to Access Safari Download Manager

The download managers show you list of items that are downloading and ones that have downloaded previously. When you attempt to download a file, a little download icon will appear at the right top corner of your screen. When you click on this icon, you will see how far the download has gone. Click on the magnifying glass beside the downloaded file to go straight to the folder where the file is, whether in the cloud or on your phone's local storage.

How to Change the Default Location for Downloads from Safari

Whenever you download content from **Safari,** it goes straight to the **Download folder** in the iCloud drive. However, you can choose to save the downloaded file in your phone's local storage with the steps below:

- From the settings app, click on **Safari.**

- Navigate to **General** and then click on **Downloads.**

- On this page, select your desired folder for saving downloaded files.

How to Auto Close Open Tabs in Safari on iOS 13

For several users, when you launch the Safari browser, you will several open tabs showing different items from social media posts to Quora to Google searches. For most of these opened tabs, you may not go back to them, but it could be quite bothersome to have to close each tab individually. The good news is that there is now a feature that can automatically close open tabs in the Safari browser after a defined time. The steps below will show you how to manage the option.

- From the settings app, click on **Safari.**

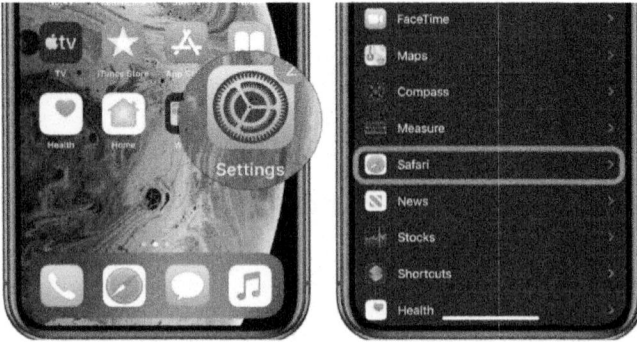

- Among the available options, go to **Tabs** then click on **Close Tabs.**

- The next screen will show a timeline for open tabs to close. The default chosen option is **"Manually."**

- You can pick from the other options if you desire: **After One Week, After One Day or After One Month.**

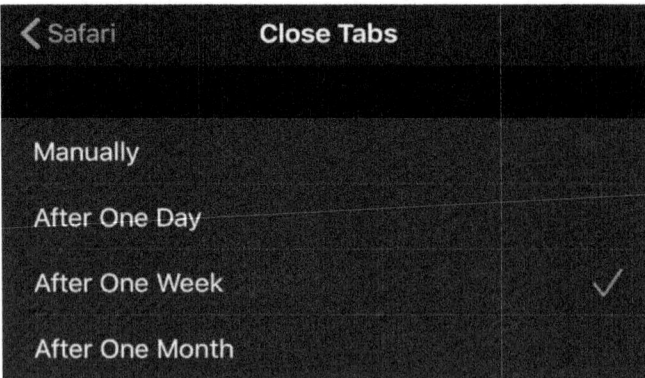

- Choose the option that will best suit your needs as there are no right or wrong options.

How to Choose When Downloaded File List is Cleared

Your Safari browser now has a Download manager in the mobile version similar to what we have in Windows and Mac. By default, the list clears at the end of each day, but you can set the device to clear the list as soon as the download is completed or manually clear the list.

- From the settings app, click on **Safari.**

- Click on **Downloads.**
- Select **Remove Download List Items**.
- Make your pick from the three available options on your screen: Upon successful download, After one day, or Manually.

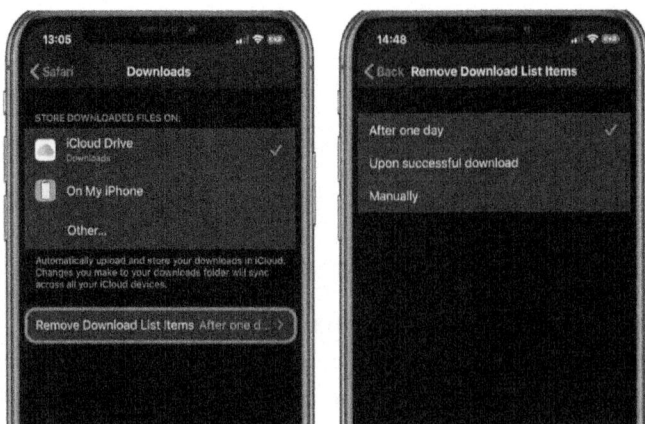

How to Modify Where Downloaded Files from Safari are Saved

By default, all downloaded files are saved in the **Download folder** of the Files app, but you can modify this by selecting an alternative storage location with the steps below:

- Go to the settings app.
- Click on **Safari.**
- Then click on **Downloads.**

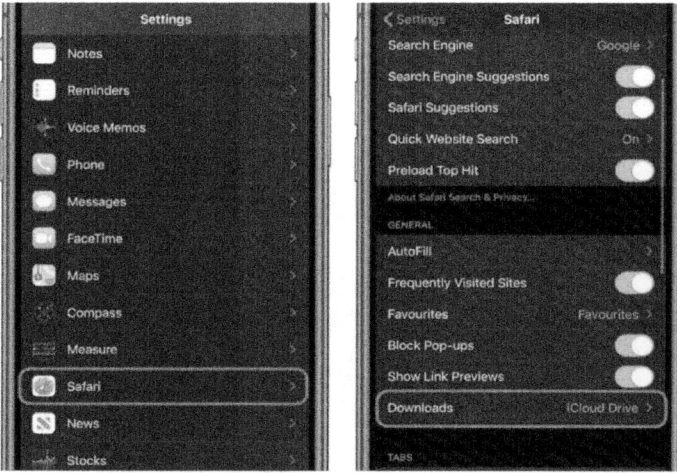

- You can then make your choice from the available options: On My iPhone, iCloud Drive, or in another location that you want.

How to Enable Content Blockers in Safari

- From the settings app, click on **Safari.**
- Then click on **Content Blockers.**

- To enable this option, move the switch beside it to the right.

Note: this option will not be available if you do not install a minimum of one 3rd party content blocker from the store.

How to Temporarily Disable Content Blockers in Safari

You use content blockers to stop ads like banners and popups from loading on webpages you visit. Content blockers are also able to disable beacons, cookies, and other features to safeguard your privacy and protect your online activities from being tracked. While this is good, there are times however that it may block a vital element like a web form. To access the web form, you will need to disable the content blocker temporarily:

- From the Safari browser, go to any website of choice.
- Click on the "aA" icon at the left top corner of your screen to show the View menu of that site.

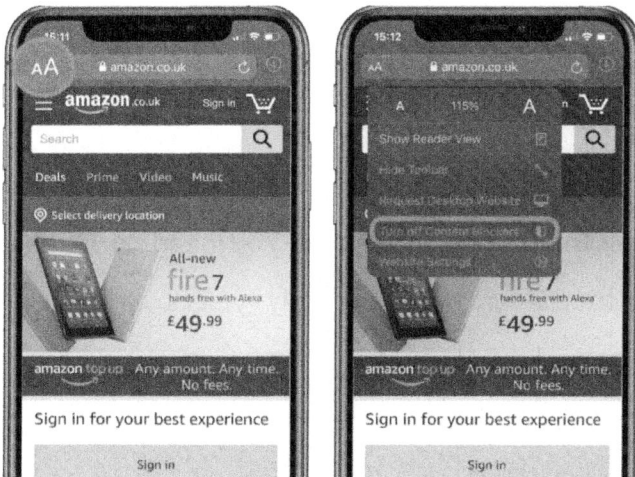

- Then click on" **Turn Off Content Blockers.**"
- To disable this feature for an individual website, click on the **Website Settings** and then move the switch beside **Use Content Blockers** to the left to disable it.

How to Share or Save a Safari Web Page as a PDF

This step is strictly for the Safari browser and does not apply to third party browsers.

- Launch the Safari browser then go to the webpage you want to save as PDF.
- Press both the Sleep/wake button and the Home button at the same time to take a screenshot.
- A preview of the screenshot will show at the left lower side of the screen.
- When you click on the preview, it will open the **Instant Markup Interface.** You need to be fast with this as you have only 5 secs before this screen disappears.
- Click on **Full-Page** in the right upper corner of the Markup interface.
- Then click on **Done** and select **Save PDF to Files** to save as a PDF file.
- Click on the **Share** button to share the PDF and choose who and how you want to share it from that screen.

List of New Keyboard Shortcuts

During the WWDC conference, Apple noted that they included about 30 new shortcuts in Safari, which has been compiled below for your reference.

- For the default font size in Reader (Cmd + 0)
- Increase Reader text size (Cmd + +)
- Decrease Reader text size (Cmd + -)
- Actual size (Cmd + 0)
- Toggle downloads (Cmd + Alt)
- Open link in background (Cmd + tap)
- Open link in new tab (Cmd + Shift + tap)
- Open link in new window (Cmd + Alt + tap)
- New Private tab (Cmd + Shift + N)
- Close other tabs (Cmd + Alt + W)
- Save webpage (Cmd + S)
- Zoom out (Cmd + -)
- Email this page (Cmd + I)
- Use selection for Find (Cmd + E)
- Zoom in (Cmd + +)
- Focus Smart Search field (Cmd + Alt + F)
- Close web view in app (Cmd + W)
- Change focused element (Alt + tab)

- To download linked file (Alt + tap)
- Add link to your Reading List (Shift + tap)
- Paste without formatting content (Cmd + Shift + Alt + V)
- To toggle bookmarks (Cmd + Alt + 1)
- Navigate around screen (arrow keys)
- Open search result (Cmd + Return)

How to Join a Wi-fi Network

- Go to Settings, then click on Wi-fi.
- Move the switch beside **Wi-fi** to the right to put on the Wi-fi.
- Select your Wi-fi network from the drop-down.
- Type in the password and click on **Join.**

How to Control Wi-fi Setup

- From the top right side of the screen, draw down the screen.
- Click on the Wi-fi icon to enable or disable.
- Move the switch beside **Wi-fi** to the right or left to put off or on.

How to Control Mobile Data

- Go to **Mobile Data** under **Settings.**

- Move the switch beside **Mobile Data** to the right or left to put off or on.
- Scroll to where you have the applications and move the switch beside each app to the right or left to put off or on.

How to Control Data Roaming

- Go to **Mobile Data** under **Settings**.
- Click on **Mobile Data Options.**
- Move the switch beside **Data Roaming** to the right or left to put off or on.

How to use your iPhone as a Hotspot

- Go to **Personal Hotspot** under **Settings**.
- Move the switch beside **Personal Hotspot** to the right or left to put off or on.
- IF wi-fi is disabled, click **Turn on Wi-fi and Bluetooth.**
- Select **Wi-fi and USB only** if wi-fi is enabled already.
- Input the wi-fi password beside the field for a wi-fi password.

- Select **Done** at the top of the screen.

How to Control Automatic Use of Mobile Data

- Go to **Mobile Data** under **Settings**.
- Move the switch beside **Wi-fi Assist** to the right or left to put off or on.

Chapter 8: Battery Tips

How to Set Optimized Battery Charging

The iOS 13 gives the option to optimize your battery charging to help the battery lasts for a longer time.

- From the settings app on your smartphone, click on **Battery.**
- Click on **Battery Health.**

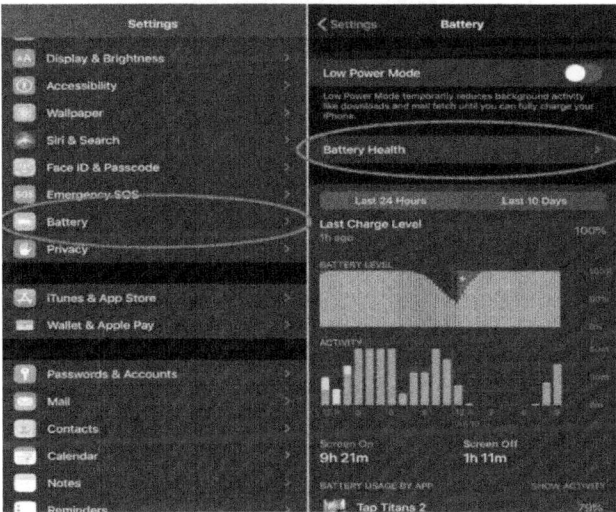

- On the next screen, you will see data showing the maximum battery capacity for your phone battery, an indication of the level of degradation, and the option to enable **Optimized Battery Charging**.

- Navigate to **Optimized Battery Charging** and move the switch to the right to enable this feature.

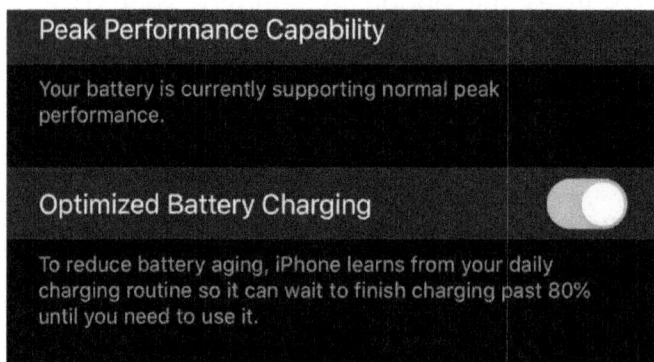

Peak Performance Capability

Your battery is currently supporting normal peak performance.

Optimized Battery Charging

To reduce battery aging, iPhone learns from your daily charging routine so it can wait to finish charging past 80% until you need to use it.

Most users of the iPhone are aware that with all the several functions that the iPhone offers, it has tendencies to zap the battery life quickly. I have compiled list of things you can do to save your battery life. It's important to note that you do not need to perform all the tips stated here, pick a few that you are okay with.

How to Stop Background Apps Refresh

One feature built to make your iPhone not only smart but also ready for you to use when needed is the Background App Refresh. The work of this feature is to look out for apps that you use often and the period in the day that you use these apps and then carry out automatic updates on the app so that you can have the latest information the next time you launch these apps. Follow the steps below to disable this feature on your smartphone.

- Go to the settings app and click on **General.**
- Then click on **Background App Refresh**.
- Move the slider to the left to disable this feature for the whole apps or disable the feature for select apps.

How to Disable Auto Update of Apps

You may have set up the option to automatically update your apps as soon as there is a new version, and this can drain the battery life. Follow the steps below to disable this feature and manually update your apps.

- From the settings app, click on the **iTunes & App Store**.
- Click on the button beside **Updates** to disable the auto app update feature.

Disable Auto App Suggestions

This feature makes use of your location service to discover your area and suggest apps that you may need based on your location. While it is a cool feature, it can, however, drain the battery. The steps below will show you how to disable the feature.

- Make a swipe down gesture from the screen top to launch the Notification center.
- Go to the **Today View** by swiping to the left.
- Navigate to the end of the screen and then click on **Edit.**
- Select the red icon beside the Siri App Suggestions.
- Click on **Remove,** then click on **Done.**

Enable Auto-Brightness

The auto-brightness feature makes your phone to adjust its brightness based on available lights in the surrounding. The feature will save you battery life as it controls the energy used on the phone.

- From the settings app, click on **General.**
- Then click on **Accessibility.**
- Select **Display Accommodations**.
- Then use the **Auto-Brightness** button

Reduce Screen Brightness

The brighter your screen is, the more power it consumes. You can control your phone's brightness using the slider on your iPhone. When you need to save battery, ensure that the brightness of the screen is at its lowest.

- From the settings app, click on **Display & Brightness**
- Then use the slider to reduce the brightness by pulling to the left.

Stop Motion and Animations

Although this feature is cool, however, disabling it will help to save battery life.

- From the settings app, click on **General.**
- Then click on **Accessibility.**

- Select **Reduce Motion.**
- Move the slider beside **Reduce Motion** to enable it.

Disable Wi-Fi When Not in Use

When not using the Wi-Fi connection, it is advisable to disable it, so it does not drain your battery.

- From the settings app, click on **Wi-Fi.**
- Then move the slider beside **Wi-Fi** to disable it.

You can also disable **Wi-Fi** through the control center. Go to the control center and click on the **Wi-Fi** button until it turns grey.

Locate the Battery Draining Apps

You can find apps using a significant percentage of your battery through a feature called the Battery Usage. Follow the steps below to use this step

- From settings app, click on **Battery**
- The apps will be displayed according to the battery usage.

- At times, there may be notes under each app to show reasons the app consumed so much battery and how to fix it.

Ensure that Personal Hotspot is Disabled

When the hotspot is on, your iPhone becomes a hotspot that shares its cellular data with other devices in range. While it can be useful, it can also drain your battery. Whenever you are done with the hotspot, it is important to remember to disable it.

- Go to the settings app.
- Click on **Personal Hotspot**
- Disable the option using the button beside it.

Disable Bluetooth

Bluetooth is another function that transmits data wirelessly and drains battery while doing so. To save your battery life, then I will advise that you put on Bluetooth only when needed. To either disable or enable your device Bluetooth, go to settings, and click on **Bluetooth.**

Disable Location Services

The iPhone comes with a built-in GPS, which is quite helpful for locating nearby restaurants, stores, etc. as well as finding directions. This app needs to send data over a network that usually tells on the battery of your device. Whenever you are not making use of the location services, you can disable it with the steps below:

- Go to the settings app.
- Click on **Privacy.**
- Then select **Location Services**.
- Toggle the button beside **Location Services** and then click on **Turn Off** to disable the option.
- Alternatively, you can navigate down the screen to select apps that should not have access to location services.

Disable Cellular Data

Similar to the Bluetooth, when using the 4G, 5G, LTE, and other cellular connections that have fast transfer speeds, they tend to drain your phone battery faster. They even consume more power when you are using it heavily, like when making HD calls or streaming videos. I know that the cellular data is essential, which is why you should disable it only when you need to save battery life.

- From the settings app, click on **Cellular.**
- Go to **Cellular Data** and move the switch to the left to disable.

Note: Turning off cellular data will not affect your Wi-Fi connection.

Disable Data Push

You may have configured the email settings to automatically download messages to your smartphone as soon as they get to the email server. It is crucial to be current on your email folder; however, when you continuously download like this, it can drain your battery faster. I will advise that rather than the automatic update, you can go to the Mail app and then manually refresh the app to receive new messages. The steps below will show you how to disable the data push feature:

- From the settings app, click on **Passwords & Accounts.**
- Or go to **Mails** from the settings app and click on **Accounts.**
- Then click on **Fetch New Data.**
- Go to **Push** and move the switch to the left to disable.

Set Emails to Download on Schedule

If you do not want to manually refresh your email, you can schedule the emails to download at a specified time. This is a balance between the two steps above, while you will not have to manually refresh your mail app, you will also not get instant update and still achieve the end goal, which is to save battery life. You can follow the steps below to set this up

- From the settings app, click on **Passwords & Accounts.**
- Then click on **Fetch New Data.**
- Navigate to the bottom and choose your options. The longer the time between checks, the longer your battery life is preserved.

Set up the Screen to Auto-Lock Sooner

Auto-locking your screen helps to save your battery life as it gives your phone a black screen. As long as your phone has something it is displaying, it will be taking out of the battery life. While I will advise that you select any of the options that suit you but do not choose **Never** as that will drain your battery life.

- From the settings app, click on **Display & Brightness**.
- Then click on **Auto-Lock**.
- You can either select any of the options from 30 seconds to 5 minutes.

Disable Fitness Tracking

The fitness tracking feature on the iPhone is used to track your steps as well as other fitness activities. It is very beneficial, especially when you are trying to get into shape, but this app also drains battery. You can disable the feature whenever you are not using it.

- From the settings app, click on **Privacy.**

- Then select **Motion & Fitness**.

- Move the switch beside **Fitness Tracking** to the left to disable this feature.

Disable AirDrop When Not in Use

AirDrop is the wireless file sharing feature of the Apple devices. To use Airdrop, you need to enable both Bluetooth and Wi-Fi and prepare your phone to locate other airdrop enabled devices. This makes use of more battery, and it is advisable to disable when not in use.

- Go to the control center, then click on **AirDrop.**

- Click on **Receiving Off** to disable the feature.

- You can also go to settings, click on **General,** then select **AirDrop**

Disable Automatic Upload of Photos to iCloud

Each time you attempt to upload data, it makes use of more battery. It is better to manually upload data than setting up an automatic upload of data. The photo app is set to automatically upload your photos to your device's iCloud account. Disable the auto-uploads and attempt to upload only when you have a full battery or when moving from your computer. Follow the steps below to check if your photos are always uploaded to iCloud.

- Go to the settings app.
- Click on **Photos.**
- Then click on **iCloud Photos**

Avoid Sending Diagnostic Data to Developers or Apple

The diagnostic data tell the developer or Apple how your smartphone is performing or not performing to help them produce better products, and so you have the option to enable this feature when setting up your device. Whenever you need to save battery life, you can follow the steps below to disable this option.

- Go to the settings app.
- Click on **Privacy.**
- Then go to **Analytics** and shift the sliders to the left to disable this feature.

Disable Vibrations

When you place your device on vibration, the phone vibrates at every notification that comes into the device. The whole process involved in this causes the battery life to go low, and if you have enabled your alert tone or ringtone then you do not need this option. Follow the steps below to turn off vibrations:

- Go to the settings app.
- Click on **Sounds & Haptics**
- Then move the slider beside **Vibrate on Ring** to the left to disable.

Other Helpful Tips to Improve the Longevity of Your iPhone Battery

Several factors can reduce the life of your battery, like leaving your phone plugged in even after the battery is fully charged. I have compiled the list below to help you prolong your battery life.

- Do not wait for your battery to drain before charging it. It is more advisable that the phone does not go below 20 perform before its next charge.

- Do not expose the smartphone to excess heat. Avoid charging your device in a very hot environment.
- If, for any reason, you do not intend to use your phone for about a week and above, ensure that the battery goes below 80% but not below 30 percent. Then shut down the phone properly before keeping aside.
- Moving your phone quickly from a very hot to a very cold condition can affect the health of the battery.
- You do not need to always fully charge your phone at all times, as it can aid in damaging your battery.

CHAPTER 9: Troubleshooting the iPhone 11 Device

Most challenges encountered with the iPhone can easily be resolved by restarting your device. However, in this section, we will look at every possible challenge you may have with the iPhone and the solutions.

Complete iPhone Reset Guide

Most minor issues that occur with the iPhone can be resolved by restarting the device or doing a soft reset. If the soft reset fails to solve the problem, then you can carry out other resets like the hard reset and master reset. Here, you will learn how to use each of the available reset methods.

How to Restart/ Soft Reset iPhone

This is by far the most prevalent solution to many problems you may encounter on the iPhone. It helps to remove minor glitches that affect apps or iOS as well as gives your device a new start. This option doesn't delete any data from your phone, so you have your contents intact once the phone comes up. You have two ways to restart your device.

Method 1:

- Hold both the side and Volume Down (or Volume Up) keys at the same time until the slider comes up on the screen.

- Move the slider to the right for the phone to shut down.

- Press the **Side** button until the Apple logo shows on the screen.

- Your iPhone will reboot.

Method 2:

- Go to **Settings** then **General.** Click on **Shut Down.**
- This will automatically shut down the device.
- Wait for some seconds, then Hold the **Side** button to start the phone.

How to Hard Reset/ Force Restart an iPhone

There are some cases when you need to force restart your phone. These are mostly when the screen is frozen and can't be turned off, or the screen is unresponsive. Just like the soft reset, this will not wipe the data on your device. It is important to confirm that the battery isn't the cause of the issue before you begin to fore-restart.

Follow the steps below to force-restart:

- Press the **Volume Up** and quickly release.
- Press the **Volume Down** and quickly release.
- Hold down the Side button until the screen goes blank and then release the button and allow the phone to come on.

How to Factory Reset your iPhone (Master Reset)

A factory reset will erase every data stored on your iPhone and return the device to its original form from the stores. Every single data from settings to personal data saved on the phone will be deleted. You should create a backup before you go through this process. You can either backup to iCloud or iTunes. Once you have successfully backed up your data, please follow the steps below to wipe your phone.

- From the **Home** screen, click on **Settings.**
- Click on **General**.
- Select **Reset**.

- Chose the option to **Erase All Content and Settings**.
- When asked, enter your passcode to proceed.
- Click **Erase iPhone** to approve the action.

Depending on the volume of data on your phone, it may take some time for the factory reset to be completed.

Once the reset is done, you may choose to set up with the **iOS Setup Assistant/Wizard** where you can choose to restore data from a previous iOS or proceed to set the device as a fresh one.

How to Use iTunes to Restore the iPhone to factory defaults

Another alternative to reset your phone is by using iTunes. To do this, you need a computer, either Mac or Windows, that has the most current version of the iOS as well as has installed the iTunes software. A factory reset is advisable as a better solution to major issues that come up from software that wasn't solved by the soft or force restart. Although you will lose data, however, you get more problems fixed, including software glitches and bugs. Follow the guide below once all is set:

- Use the Lightning Cable or USB to connect your device to the computer.

- Open the iTunes app on the computer and allow it to recognize your device.

- Look for and click on your device from the available devices shown in iTunes.

- If needed, chose to back up your phone data to iTunes or iCloud on the computer.

- Once done, tap the **Restore** button to reset your iPhone.

- A prompt will pop-up on the screen, click **Restore** to approve your action.

- Allow iTunes to download and install the new software for your device.

I Can't Activate my Mobile Phone

There are four possible reasons for this. Causes and solutions are listed below:

- If the activation was not done correctly, repeat the activation steps as instructed in this book

- There may be a temporary problem with your network connection. Wait for some time and try again or you can move to any location and then try again.

- The problem may be with the SIM card. If so, contact your carrier's customer service for assistance.

CHAPTER 10: Conclusion

With all the teachings in this book, I am confident that you will be able to enjoy to the fullest all the fantastic features of the iPhone 11. The iPhone 11 is not only a phone for making and receiving calls. With the right knowledge on how to use the iPhone 11, you can turn it to your office and achieve greater things with this device.

If you are pleased with the content of this book, don't forget to recommend this book to a friend.

Thank you.

Printed in Great Britain
by Amazon